The Adventures of Commander Candle

The First Juncture:

Tomorrow is a Star Lit Sky

J. J. Hall,
111 Sixth Street
Scotia, NY 12302

Printed in the United States of America through Lulu.com: www.lulu.com

The Adventures of Commander Candle
The First Juncture: Tomorrow is a Star Lit Sky.

Cover design by J. J. Hall

Author's note: This is a work of fiction! Any names, characters, places, or incidents are the product of the author's imagination and used fictitiously. Any resemblance to actual persons, living or dead, events, or locales is entirely coincidental. References to the Lord is with the understanding that He operates according to His sovereign will, and are meant for the purpose of illustration and toward the end that even in a work of fiction, that we do not exclude Him from our thoughts.

ISBN#: 978-0-557-16750-0
Hall, J. J. The Adventures of Commander Candle, The First Juncture: Tomorrow is a Star Lit Sky

---

J. J. Hall is available for book signings, guest preaching and teaching and writer's workshops. Please contact him at jjhall8@yahoo.com

---

Dedication

To my wife Frances and my sons Jeremy, Andrew and James: My best stories will never compare to the family life the Lord has given us!

Acknowledgements

Its take significant love and support to bring a novel to fruition. A wise author not only tests his ideas, but also invites review. The positive response to the story serves as a never ending encouragement to keep going during the many humdrum hours required to turn an idea into a book.

While I have already praised my family in the dedication, I must credit them with both practical help and inspirational assistance. My sons, Jeremy, Andrew and James have always been the first line of experimentation. (Thankfully, for them, I am a writer. If I were a scientist, who knows what may have happened!) They have read the story, viewed artwork and have contributed significantly in helping form the plot.

I also have to credit my wife for the many sacrifices involved that allow me the time and space to dream. As a home-schooling family, the effort in running the household is no small undertaking. There is many a morning and evening my wife carried the load so I could stare at the computer. I simply could not have done this without her!

I also want to thank Jonathan Moore, who eagerly enjoyed the stories in Sunday school. His extra-ordinary interest and enthusiasm spurred further work on the story.

I appreciate the review and criticism of my good friend Mark Wright. His comments led directly to the expansion of the development of the character Espwin Daria, as well as the inclusion of the opening and closing scenes in the private investigator's office. Mark had already read the prequel to all of these adventures featuring Jeremy Hawks and encouraged me to tie Commander Candle more definitively to it. I do plan to revise this first work and release it at another juncture.

Finally, but definitively not the last to be praised, is the Lord Jesus Christ. In 1978 He confronted my selfish and sinful condition with His redemptive heart! I doubt I would not be alive today nor appreciating any prospect of eternal rest if He did not intervened to halt my self destructive ways!

Thanks to all that helped make this novel a reality!

Forward

It is never too late! **The Adventures of Commander Candle** is based upon characters created when I was thirteen years old! At this time, I am an ancient fifty five years old, a span of 42 years from the seed of an idea and its conclusion!

However, this story had its first expression as "filler" after Sunday school, when my pastor's sermon would run long! I began to use this as a "story" time. "The Adventures" became more and more interesting to my students. After a couple of weeks, I prepared the narrative before hand. Fortunately, for me, the pastor continued to work overtime! And so, the basic outline of **The Adventures of Commander Candle** was born!

The story has been expanded and a sequel has been completed. I took pause to do the editorial work for my first published novel **An Old-Fashioned, Horrible Alien Movie** (American Book Publishers 2002). I am currently working on a third installment of **The Adventures of Commander Candle.** I plan to have many more episodes, if the Lord tarries. When He comes again, there will not be a need for such a fictional work to stir our imagination!

It is exciting to offer a science fiction that labors to maintain harmony with the Holy Scriptures. Please remember, this is only meant to be edifying entertainment! Do not look to these pages for theology or any attempts to answer the question as to whether there is life out there in other corners of the universe. All I will go on record to say is if there are extraterrestrials it will be our responsibility to preach the Gospel to them! This story is not a substitute for Bible time with your children, but is intended as an alternative to watching Saturday morning cartoons, X-Box (whatever version we are up to) comic books and novels featuring pre and post pubescent witches and warlocks. This IS NOT Sunday school material, unless your pastor runs real long and you need to fill time!

However, **The Adventures of Commander Candle** is a lot of fun! I had so much writing this story and it will show as you read from page to page.

Please partake of my artistic gift, and at the end of the day, it is just an ability to tell a story bestowed upon me by the Lord. I am not a genius, or even a mildly smart man; just someone blessed enough to retain some child-like imagination in the midst of day to day living in this depraved world. As you read **The Adventures of Commander Candle,** please accept it in the spirit I offer it, one child to another asking "Can you come out to play?

CONTENTS

Chapter One: "I'll see you tomorrow"

A black gloved hand crashed into the face of the lone figure. The recipient of the fist was tied to a chair. As the victim's head rocked back, blood trickled from his lower lip. The darkened room hid the features of the three who shared this warehouse office, and who were participants in this squalid drama.

"Nick," cautioned the bystander from the shadows. He pointed to a surveillance camera on the wall. "Our benefactor wants him in one piece. The assailant walked to the door way and flicked on the light switch.

"Yeah," stated a husky ruffian with dark hair and an even darker countenance. He grimaced as he rubbed a blackened left eye as he also recoiled from a recent memory.

"I deserve to get even, Lou. Last time we met, he got the jump on me."

"That is not how I remembered it, Nick," whispered the man in tied to the chair. "You were "whupped" and it was a fair fight!"

Nick raised his gloved hand in response to the provocative statement. Lou, who was a slender man, grabbed his fist.

"Colonel Petronavich wants Hawks alive and undamaged," he cautioned once again. There was a moment in which each resorted to their own quiet thoughts. The bound man lifted his head up to reveal a boyish, blond framed face set upon a wiry and well developed physique. He was dressed in a black turtle neck with matching dark pants and a remnant of charcoal paste on his face. He was obviously captured in the midst of a "black op" and was now in an enemy's power.

"Colonel Petronavich, eh? What happened to the family, Nick? Since when does the Mafia kowtow to former KGB agents?"

"Since," interjected Lou, "You put away the last of the Luccessi leadership, Mr. Hawks. So, we have our own axe to grind with you, but the money Petronavich is paying us will help us to rebuild for the future."

"Lou Luccessi," said Hawks, "the only thing you will get from Petronavich is a bullet, like the rest of your family. He has killed more of your relatives than I put away. Quite frankly, those in the penitentiary are better off. The Russian colonel has a very poor record when it comes to paying his debts."

Nick stepped forward with a raised fist once again.

"He'll pay us, even though you won't have any teeth left in your head!"

The door suddenly flew open. A Markarov 9mm PM was aimed and fired several times. Nick's unconscious body hit the floor. A second burly Russian covered Lou with an Uzi. Between these two physical specimens, a much shorter man walked through. He had slicked brown hair and a thin, cruel face.

"I said undamaged!" he stated.

"He only slugged him once!" protested Lou Luccessi.

"I sincerely apologize," said Petronavich with a hint of sarcasm. He drew his own Markov PM from within his dark overcoat. "I will only shoot you once!"

His pistol reported and Lou fell.

"I think we have established our organization. The last of the Luccessi family has passed into history!" The former soviet colonel turned his attention to the man seated and bound.

"So this is the great Jeremy Hawks, Private Investigator," he mocked. "Under normal circumstances, I would applaud your expertise; however, these days I find your competence quite inconvenient."

"I am not sure I understand your angst," whispered the detective.

"Mr. Hawks, you are too modest! I believe that your activities greatly accelerated the fall of the Soviet Union. Because of you I must readjust to my new criminal vocation and hope that we can finance the electoral defeat of Boris Yeltsin."

"So, the KGB is back in the drug business."

"We never left it. But enough about me! I really need to know what you know, and who you have shared this knowledge with."

"That is easy. I know that you have been trying to broker nuclear technology to some of the more violent governments in the Middle East. You have been laundering money from the Arabian Peninsula for groups in Uzbekistan, and have managed to acquire an interest in the poppy fields of Afghanistan."

"You have quite a dossier on me, Mr. Hawks. Please continue!"

"I also know that there is a significant amount of C-4 stored in this warehouse. I believe that you are about to fulfill a contract for eliminating a recently former president. I am not sure how much Sadaam is paying. Was it 20 Million or Thirty?"

"I have Forty Million Euros. Sadaam is intent of converting the standard oil currency from dollars to Euros. Now, please tell me more."

"Do you mean your involvement in the Luccessi family murders, the laundering of the Middle Eastern money, the smuggling of nuclear technology…?"

"Yes, everything we have discussed," the colonel stated impatiently. "God knows I am the master architect, and I am content to keep this with Him."

Colonel Petronavich aimed his Markov PM at the detective.

"What evidence do you have?"

Like lightning, the private investigator broke through his bonds and relieved the former KGB agent of his side arm. Several FBI agents crashed though the skylight above and repelled into the room. The two body guards had law enforcement personnel cover them from behind, and they were quickly face down on the floor and restrained.

Jeremy Hawks ripped his shirt off to reveal a "wire", a recording device wound around his torso.

"How does a confession sound?"

Nick and then Lou stood up, and opened their coats so arriving EMT's could tend to the bruises left by the impact of the rounds against their bullet proof vests.

"Hawks, I'm tired of taking slugs for you!" complained "Nick".

"I'm just glad they didn't shoot me in the head!" added "Lou".

"Why? It's not like that's a vital organ for you!" quipped "Nick".

"Hardy, har har! The only thing worse than living on the edge is listening to your bad jokes!" The two undercover police were taken out by the medical personnel.

"No court in the United States will ever convict me, comrade!" Petronavich declared. As he did so, another man in a suit and tie walked in.

"I am Sam Champlain with the Department of State. Peter Petronavich, I am here to inform you will be extradited to the Republic of Georgia to fulfill a arrest warrants for murder."

"I'll be hanged!" he protested.

"If we have your confession and cooperation, Colonel Petronavich, we will be able to refuse extradition so you can serve your sentence here," encouraged an FBI agent. He was a short and balding person, the senior agent in this operation.

"Can we cooperate too?" asked one of the Russian body guards. The second nodded from his place of restraint on the floor.

"I will make the arrangements!" stated the FBI official. He looked over to the detective and delivered an assured wink.

"Let's book our catch of the day, gentlemen!" he crowed. "Great job!"

Moments later the room was cleared of felons and law enforcement alike, save for the senior FBI agent and Jeremy Hawks. The two stood up and headed out the door. Soon they were on a busy sidewalk in the Bronx.

"You have done another good job, Mr. Hawks! I wish you would simply join us so we don't have to go through the formality of contracting you."

"Jenkins, when did you offer me a contract? I have been doing these jobs pro-bono. I appreciate your professional opinion, but I have such a sense that God has something different for me."

"Events like your secret meeting tonight?" queried Jenkins.

"Phil, have you been bugging my phone again?"

"No, but your secretary contacted me. She is concerned."

"Debbie is at it again? I should fire her."

Phil laughed.

"I guess I could hire her, then. It is part of my plan. But I doubt very much you could fire your own sister."

"Don't underestimate me, Phil. Besides, sometimes I think it would be safer for her to work for the FBI."

Phil Jenkins stopped and faced the detective,

"Jeremy, what is going on?"

The sleuth became serious in his demeanor.

"Phil, I have been contacted by someone who purports to have information about my father."

The FBI agent stood in stunned silence.

"Jeremy, this is a cold case! You saw the file! I don't believe that there is anything else on Earth that would make sense out of that mess!"

"Phil, when have any of my adventures been limited to Earth?"

* * *

It was late at night. From the boulevard, the Park Avenue building was just a dark shadow, save for the lone window that remained lit. Two figures approached. They were bundled against the cold wintry chill of the New York City streets. The lead was distinctly feminine. She nodded to her hulking companion. He was bundled up in a manner that would disguise his features. She pointed to the illuminated office above. Her companion nodded back.

She sported a carrying case, which she clung to. From this she removed a device. This was inserted into the security keypad. The door yielded to the electronic persuasion. Within moments, they were inside.

The elevator opened up to a dim hallway. The two came to a glass door. It read "Jeremy Hawks, Private Investigations" and had a picture of an osprey holding a fish. The woman's face wrinkled as she smiled. She pushed through the door.

The detective sat behind an oak desk. His blond hair was disheveled and his chin unshaven. It had been a long day! Now, anxiety was painted across his face. The woman turned off the light and sat down opposite him. Her companion stood by the door, an obvious move to insure secrecy.

"You claim to have information concerning my father?" the sleuth asked.

"I do", the woman stated.

"How did you come by this information?"

"I will disclose this after I present what I have."

"And what is the price?"

"After you see my presentation, I am sure this discussion will", she paused to take a breath, "take its natural course."

"And why is your companion here?"

"The nature of this disclosure requires the use of technology that cannot fall into the wrong hands. I am sure you can understand that?"

“Yes, I have had more than my share of being exposed to technology in the wrong hands.”

“Yes, I have heard! You saved a secret military space shuttle, the McArthur II, and had to fight off spies, a secret society, aliens and robots to do it!”

“Let’s get on with it,” the private investigator broke in impatiently.

The woman removed a wafer thin screen from her carrying case. She placed this upon the wall. It seemed to adhere by itself. Then it expanded several times its size.

“Time to watch a movie”, she said warmly, “a vintage piece from 1969. I call it ‘This is your life, Jeremy Hawks”.

* * *

“I’ll see you tomorrow.”

“Daddy, I want you to stay”, pouted the young boy. His long flaxen locks trickled in the autumn breeze. His blue eyes were moist from disappointment.

“Your father has work to do at the college”, stated his mother as she swooped out to the front porch to rescue her husband. “We will have plenty of time tomorrow.”

"No we won't", the boy cried. He ran into the house and up the stairs. Finding his bed he flung himself upon it, but its gentle folds could not comfort him. His heart pained him, and he could not explain why. All he knew was that he wanted to keep his dad home.

Back by the front steps his parents studied one another. The wiry built father ran his hand through his balding scalp. The neatly trimmed sides of his head were sprinkled with premature gray, granting him an air of dignity. He peered at his wife through thick oval rimmed glasses. These would occasionally reflect his wife's red hair, as they moved their heads in conversation. They stood quietly, as if examining the quiet neighborhood's surroundings. The ranch houses were lined up in silent testimony to the inactivity within them.

"He's right, you know," she said. "Ever since you took that grant, it seems like this project is more important than he is. I am beginning to feel that way, too. I guess he is vocalizing our frustration over not being together."

"I know. I know. I'm just so close with this break through! It's going to be a quantum leap in the physical sciences, darling. I believe that I am about to open a doorway into many other worlds!"

"That may be fine for you, and for everyone else. But will it be worth it if you lose your, whole family? You haven't had a meal with us during your experiments; haven't played with the kids; haven't spent any time with me. You haven't even come to church! What good is it if you gain the whole world and lose your soul? What's wrong with staying home today? You haven't taken a day off for over three months."

"But I'm so close! So close!"

"But we are not! You have been saying 'tomorrow' for a long time now. You're missing the point! You just said tomorrow again to your son. He doesn't believe you anymore."

The father looked ashamed as he glanced upward toward his son's room.

"I can't cancel out on today's experiments. But you're right. I need a break. The kids and you need me. I better take some time off."

"Please. Ever since you have been on this project, this man…" she paused to search her memory for his name.

"Tweed," reminded her husband.

"This Mr. Tweed has you totally on his agenda. The way he drives you and the project has been very harmful to us, Jeremiah. I am handling everything at home, and alone. We have a five year old with an abundance of energy, and I just had twin. They're coming up on a year. I need you! They need you! Besides, I keep having this creepy feeling like we are being watched, even when you aren't here."

"Everything is going to be fine. I doubt that there are any spies in town. Western New York is hardly the venue for international intrigue."

The husband and wife embraced.

"Let me get to work. The sooner I'm there, the sooner I'll be home!"

After conveying this promise, he squeezed into a VW Beetle and drove away. His wife waved, and then turned to walk inside.

* * *

A light haired assistant continued his study of the device in front of him. He was in a massive workshop that also had a small observatory with additional skylights for evening star gazing. It had an antiquated telescope that matched the older brick building, but was accommodating enough to the 100 level astronomy courses available at the college.

The intern examined power couplings. He looked at prints that were on a drafting table. He grinned with satisfaction as he viewed page after page.

"Today's the day we make history!" he said.

"That's what I am paying you two for." snapped a gruff voice from behind. The assistant turned to greet his "benefactor".

"Mr. Tweed, I didn't hear you come in!"

“It's been three months, Collins. I expect results!"

"Yes sir, Professor Hawks has everything under control. I believe that today's test will help us isolate the wavelength of the energy expression the Professor has developed."

"How is that going to help us, Collins? This is all fun stuff to the pencil heads in the world, but what applications do you foresee? What's in it for me?"

"First of all, our discovery will amplify existing energy transfers. Amplify them exponentially! Imagine being able to convert gasoline into mechanical energy within the confines of one of our energy fields. Instead of 20 to 30 miles per gallon, consider the possibility of thousands of miles per gallon.

"Likewise, atomic energy can be used to power space flight. In time, our discovery will enable both high speeds and long ranges for the atomic fuels used to date. Future development will, of course, make the stars reachable! Perhaps, even in our lifetime!"

"I like it when you talk cosmic, Collins. Believe me, I would trade all of my money for a visit to the stars! Earth is a bit too boring for me these days!"

"I am not sure I can give you the stars today", echoed a voice from the doorway, "but how about an economical habitat on the moon?" It was the boy's father.

"That's what I like about you Professor Hawks. You're the practical one around here," said Tweed. "When's 'show time'?"

"Let's start the countdown. I should be able to have a good spectrum analysis by two o'clock. To do that, we will need to have our energy expression converting an electromagnetic field by one. I think we can do this today".

"How are we going to maintain field integrity? Are you sure the effect will be stable?" asked Collins.

"We have seen our energy expression stabilize radioactive strontium, carbon 14, and even deuterium. If we can convert and contain alpha particles, beta particles and gamma waves, I think converting a simple magnetic field should be do-able.

"What do you mean by stabilizing nuclear energy?" Tweed asked.

"I have illustrated with our experiments with Carbon 14, and Strontium. These elements emit nuclear energy, being mindful of the small amounts we have worked with, were converted by our energy expression into a useable stream of force. The negative characteristics of these forms of radiation were "nullified". In theory, our discovery could even be used as the ultimate missile defense!"

"Nuclear arms obsolete!" Collins stated with pride. "Peace in our time!"

"Spoken like a true idealist," Tweed commented. "A good history class will tell you that we are a conquering race. I'm sure we'll find another way to duke it out even if we don't nuke it out."

"In any event, Collins and I will begin preparing our experiment. If you come back after lunch, there is a good chance that we may make some history for you."

"Always the wit, Mr. Hawks; I'll be back at one."

"Tweed left. The professor followed the fat man's progress as he came to his Rolls Royce. A rough looking driver met him and they both nodded in the direction of the laboratory.

"That guy gives me the willies, Ted. He scares me; especially how he drives the project forward."

"Progress is often funded in the most unusual way" stated Ted.

"Give me one example", challenged the professor. Collins thought hard for a minute.

"Your time is up. Be sure to exclude that kind of reasoning from your thesis presentation. I don't mean to get negative on the project. This pace has been hard on my family. I really need a couple of weeks off."

"But professor, we are about to make history!"

"Collins, what is history without family?"

"In my house, you get left alone!" Ted said laughing.

"And if you're not a selfish person, it is the worse thing that could happen."

"I guess one man's heaven is another man's hell," Collins commented in an attempt to make light of Professor Hawk's concerns.

"Hell isn't something joke about, Ted. Some people hate God so much; they would just rather live there. I have no intention of ending up like that no matter what scientific break through happens today."

"Okay, okay! If we make history today, I'll go to church with you on Sunday. Let's get on with it."

The two men busied themselves with their preparations.

*   *   *

Tweed greedily chewed his sandwich as he sat at a restaurant table. His driver stood beside him and listened attentively to his boss between his mouthfuls of food.

"If the experiment succeeds have the boys bring the “laser projector” to the lab tonight. Let’s have an open line to the observatory ready. We'll try a dry run to see if the astrophysicists on my payroll have been earning their money. Let's detain Collins to run the thing. I believe that we can have our way with him, especially if it becomes clear that he has no other choice."

"What about Professor Hawks?"

"I do not think that we can work with him. He has too many," Tweed sought his memory for the right word, "morals." Make it look like an accident.

"I got ya, boss. There have been a lot of fires around here lately. These houses made in the forties need to have the electrical wiring upgraded."

Both men laughed heartlessly. While it was only business, planning he professor’s demise brought a dark pleasure to them.

*   *   *

"It went great, Darling! Great!" the professor crowed over the telephone. He was placing files and his noted into a briefcase, one reminiscent of a grade school “book-bag”. He continued his conversation with his wife.

"On top of everything else, I will be getting a couple of weeks off. I promise you that it will be pure catch up time. "

He paused to listen to her encouraging words.

"Sweetheart, I really look forward to the time. I really do. I'm finally going to give our boy a tomorrow. What's that? There is someone's at the door? Why would someone be there at this hour? You better get it, it must be important! I will tell you the rest when I get home."

Jeremiah Hawks hung up the telephone.

It was past eight o'clock when the professor concluded his journal entry. With a sigh of relief he closed the book. He placed this last item into his attaché case. He stood up from his desk and walked out into the hall. He removed a large key from his pocket, and inserted it into the keyhole to lock his office door. He turned down the corridor to hasten his way home.

At that moment, he paused as he heard a low hum from the lab. He retraced his steps so he could listen more intently. Realizing that there was some activity, he quickly walked to the laboratory. He froze in disbelief at the doorway.

Collins was at the controls. Tweed looked on with several other men who stood along side the industrialist with their arms folded to their chest.

'What's the meaning of this!" protested Professor Hawks.

"Increase the power,” Tweed commanded.

"You don't know what you are doing!" the scientist protested.

"But I do, professor. I do. You see, I am not as unlearned as you suspect. Today's experiment enabled us to measure the wave characteristics of your energy expression. My resident astrophysicists have been able to detect similar wave characteristics using our radio telescope and radiographic detection device. We discovered these in the Crab Nebula."

“Which means?"

"Professor this means that there is life out there. If your energy expression is as exponentially accelerating as I suspect, we should be able to pass a laser through your field and, with that projection device, aim it at a similar energy source.”

The scientist looked on as two technicians began to run power cables to a tripod mounted laser. This was aimed at a collector, which had optical cables that fed to the main “projector”. This had the appearance of a mirror of sorts that rested on a platform on the floor. This in turn had a broad access to the night sky through the opened observatory ceiling.

"Like a homing beacon!" Collins exclaimed. .

"We won't have to go to them, Hawks. They will come to us!" Tweed laughed maniacally.

"But, Tweed! Just because we have not known about this energy expression, does not mean that it must be manufactured. It could occur naturally. Electricity occurs naturally, but it is only within this century that we have learned how to harness it and apply it."

"I am willing to bet you're life that this is not a natural phenomenon." Two men grasped the professor and held him fast.

“You will not need this anymore,” stated Tweed as he relieved Jeremiah Hawks of his briefcase.

"What are you planning to do, Mr. Tweed?" asked Collins.

"You will continue your work, boy," commanded the industrialist, "or you will find out first hand!"

Sheepishly, Ted Collins returned to his activity. Occasionally he would glance over. For the most part, he did exactly as Tweed told him.

"I don't believe that I can work with you any more, Professor Hawks. Let's hope that the 'Star Trek' theory of beaming people up is possible. You're about to go where no man has gone before!"

The ruffians held the scientist fast as a third taped his mouth. A technician stepped forward to give Tweed his progress report.

"According to our best telemetry, we will need to wait until ten thirty tonight. Then we can make our shot."

"Excellent," Tweed said. "I guess tonight we will make history!" He nodded to a figure hidden in the shadows. It was his driver. He stepped forward. "No witnesses. None, at all!"

The driver nodded back then left.

Bound and gagged, the professor prayed.

"Lord Jesus," Jeremiah Hawks he cried in silence, “I don't care what happens to me. Please protect my family."

*   *   *

The scientist's residence was ablaze. Billowing smoke seemed to erase the starlit sky. The loud roar of a fire out of control was drowning out the siren sounds of the engines answering the call for assistance.

The door burst open. Jeremiah Hawks' son came running from the front porch, with his twin brother and sister in his small arms. All adrenaline, he clasped them tightly, and would not allow the attending firefighters to relieve him of his burden. Finally, the lad surrendered them, just as he, himself fell to his knees and cried.

Smoke swirled all around as the flames quickly reduced the home

"We've got the kids!" the fireman called. He motioned for the paramedics who attended to the children. He rose and spoke to his chief.

That five year old saved his brother and sister!" he exclaimed. His face shone with amazement. "He's unreal! He got his baby brother and sister out all by himself!"

"Where are the parents?" asked the Fire Chief.

"I don't know. If they were in there, they did not make it out", he said grimly.

"Better tell the sheriff. I guess we need to get Social Services here. If we don't find some relatives, these kids could end up split three ways!"

"Yeah," said the fireman, "but it sure beats being dead!"

* * *

The laser shot into the collector and the projector beamed heavenward in a spectacular show illuminating the night sky conspicuously. Passing through the professor's field generator produced the desired effect as Tweed's technicians were in awe of the demonstration. Collins stood transfixed, as he too found the display too dramatic to retain a consciousness of his personal peril.

"Professor, we did it! We are making our first contact with another world."

"Take the tape off," Tweed commanded. "What do you have to say for yourself, professor? According to our telemetry report we have joined our energy beam with theirs! What do you think of that?"

"I don't, Tweed. You are just another selfish person who wants to rob one of God's wonders and turn it to fulfill your own fantasy."

"And what fantasy is that, Mr. Hawks?"

"That there is no God who will hold you accountable for your actions or that you will find some life in space to validate this illusion."

"If I am such a wicked man, why was my money good enough for you?"

"Simple. I was so blinded by my sense of achievement that I allowed you to deceive me."

"Well, boo-hoo, that's a sad story. I'll make sure that does not happen again! Boys, place the professor in the energy field. It's time for him to meet God, his or mine!" Tweed laughed cruelly.

One of his technicians glanced up. He had a concerned expression.

"What is it?" asked Tweed.

"Sir, the beam we have projected into space seems to be on a parabolic course! We do not have a straight line!"

"What does that mean?" asked Tweed. Jeremiah Hawks answered.

"It means that outer space may be smaller than we have imagined, Tweed. To me it is just more proof that God created the universe."

"Nice bluff, Hawks. I'm sending you anyway!"

"Mr. Tweed?" interrupted the technician, "He may be correct. And that would also mean that the speed of light is not constant. While we have indeed seemed to make contact with a similar energy source, I can't guarantee that we have 'homed in" on anything significant. We are making a blind shot!"

"Doctor Cicada, allow me to remind you that I am aware that your first PhD was in entomology. While I appreciate your work on this project, when I want your advice on developing pesticides, I will ask it. When I require advice on the cosmos, I prefer that you remain silent! Now throw him in!"

As they moved the professor forward, Tweed's technician's eyes met his. His anger was clearly evident as he pushed past the bound academic.

"Just get out of here!" whispered the Jeremiah Hawks. "I'll create a distraction! Just save my family!"

The technician nodded. He moved quickly to the back of the room, and stood by the door.

The professor suddenly drove hard toward the laser. Ted Collins moved to prevent his mentor from his intentions. Both tumbled into the energy field fueled by the intersecting laser. But instead of being instantly vaporized, they found themselves contained within the field on the projector. They examined themselves in wonderment. As hard as they tried, however, they could not push through to escape the beam. Tweed looked on; his jaw slung wide open in disbelief.

“The laser’s effects have been ‘nullified’! They are alive within the light beam!” declared the industrialist.

Then, suddenly, Ted Collins and Professor Jeremiah Hawks were drawn up the shaft of light. They were gone!

"Did you see that?" Tweed exclaimed. "Did you see that?"

"I can't explain it sir!" another technician stated.

"I can. Those two were taken away by the signal we over lapped. They are on another world!" Tweed exclaimed. He was mesmerized. He began to walk toward the energy field.

"Sir, the telemetry's has been changed warned another technician. Even if they have been sent to another civilization, I can't guarantee that you will arrive there."

The protest went unheeded. Tweed walked into the energy field.

Unexpectedly there was an arc of electrical power that flew from a control panel to the mounted laser. Tweed cast a fearful glance as sparks flashed all through the laboratory. As smoke filled the room, technicians and Tweed's protectors lost sight of their boss. Without any apparent explanation the laser, still amplified by the energy field, swung in the tripod downward then in a circular motion. It sliced through wall, desks and equipment. Screams of panic filled the air just as thick clouds of acrid vapors caused by the combustion filled the lab. The horror was cut short by a large explosion. Smoke bricks and I-beams were tossed into the air. Each of the dense objects fell ungracefully to the ground.

A lone Chevy Nova was idling a short distance from the campus. Doctor Cicada stood and observed the fire left by the blast. He held fast a brief case, filled with the scientist’s notes. His face revealed the heart’s struggle within.

“I’m holding a gold mine,” he said to himself, “or even more than that! It will bring more than enough to fund my own research!”

He lifted the case to his breast, as if to hug it affectionately. His expression hardened. “I’ll show Tweed that I have a little more going for me than developing pesticides!”

In short order, he was inside his automobile, and dove away.

*   *   *

"When are you going to get here? We need help!" exclaimed the fire chief into the radio. "It's the second alarm for my boys tonight. We're exhausted and this fire at the college is out of control!"

He paused for an answer.

"We'll do our best! Just get here!" he declared.

Another fire fighter approached.

"Westfield and Brockton called in. They are on the way. Even Silver Creek is sending trucks!"

"These are two of the worse fires I've ever seen: and in one night!"

"The fire marshal is listing the Hawks residence fire as suspicious."

"I expected that. I bet this one is too. Up there is Professor Hawks' laboratory. It's too much of a coincidence."

Two men in plain cloths approached the fire chief.

"What now?" he asked."The men flashed their badges.

"I'm Trent Jones, FBI. This is Investigator Laramie of the Department of Defense. Once the fire is contained we have been authorized to cordon off the area and begin our investigation."

"I understand. I'll have my men out of your way as soon as possible."

"Are there any survivors?" asked Laramie.

"Not here. I have three kids who survived the earlier fire."

"What earlier fire?" asked Jones.

"There was one at the residence of the college professor. The same professor works in this building".

Both agents exchanged a puzzled look.

"Do you have the address?" asked Laramie.

The fire chief nodded. He scribbled the location on a small note pad he retrieved from inside his coat. He handed this to the FBI agent.

"You have been very helpful" stated Jones.

"Any time, we're not going anywhere at the moment"

The two men left.

"What was that about?" asked the second firefighter.

"It sounds like trouble with a capital "T". Let's get this fire under control. We'll let them sort out the mess that's left."

*   *   *

Young Jeremy Hawks sat sullenly in the hospital ER with a blanket wrapped around his shoulders. Occasionally, he would muster enough emotional energy to sob, but this quickly gave way to the silence of despair. A tall, middle aged woman hurriedly approached and picked up a chart at the receiving desk.

"What do we have, Kate?" she asked the nurse.

"That five year old boy, over there, and his two eleven month old twin brother and sister. They survived a fire at their home. The mother has not been found. His father was at the college where his laboratory suffered an explosion. He has not been found, either."

"That is awfully suspicious!"

"The Feds are in the cafeteria. They spent an hour talking to the boy, Norma. Like the kid needed to be grilled! He just lost his parents!"

"Has he been seen by a doctor?"

"Yes, he was, but only long enough to be sure that he could be seen by law enforcement."

"Let's get him examined, and he and the twins cleared for release. I'm taking them home tonight. I have temporary foster parents lined up, three couples who will be sensitive to the trauma they have experienced. That will give me time to establish permanent placements."

The social worker began to walk briskly down the hall.

"Norma Allen, where are you going?"

"I plan to have a word with the "Feds". I don't care what crime has been committed. I should have been here an hour ago!"

* * *

Norma was on the phone.

"I have three kids, darling. They survived the fire. Let's put them in Jason's room, since he is at boot camp. The mom and dad are gone, presumed dead from simultaneous accidents at their home and at the college where he worked. The FBI told me that they have uncovered a body in the basement of the home. He was some guy's driver, and he had a criminal record! Right now, the Department of Defense is scouring the lab building, so my guess is that the professor was working on something top secret."

There was muffled speaking evident trough the headset.

'It should not be a problem. I know Kerri is his age, so having her around may be a good distraction for him. I know our daughter is exuberant, but I am sure he will appreciate the company. It is only for a couple of days."

Norma paused to listen.

"I know! If he is cute she'll want to marry him! Rob, they are only five! Ten years from now, we can worry about that!"

He husband spoke again.

"No we can't keep them! We are going to be living on your pastor's salary, soon. As long as I am working for DSS, I can't participate in any foster care of adoptions, anyway! If they are assigned to anyone we know you could end up being their minister."

*   *   *

Laramie and Jones stood amidst the smoking wreckage that was once the laboratory of Jeremiah Hawks. A colonel in the air force approached.

"No notes, no bodies; I just can't wait to try and write this report!" he complained.

"What happened?" asked Jones.

"To the best of my knowledge, the experiment was a success!" said Laramie. "We have a massive explosion and no radiation! Too bad, no one lived through it to tell about it."

"Then this one will end up as a cold case," lamented Jones.

"Yeah," agreed Laramie. "And DOD will have to pick up the tab for a new building!"

Chapter Two: Ground Zero!

The darkened living room was not very elaborate. A reclining chair faced a television screen dancing with images. A refrigerator door could be heard opening and then shutting in the other room. A shadow passed in the lit kitchen, as a voice mumbled about the location of a glass. It was a scene that is probably acted out a million times each day in the good old USA.

The figure returned from the kitchen. His squat and plump frame was further accented by the pale, turquoise skin on his hands and his face. His hair was thick, black and short, standing up on end like a crew cut of sorts. His front bangs were formed into a decided triangular shape that almost intersected thick, bushy eyebrows.

This creature waddled back onto his easy chair to eat the sandwich he had made, followed by copious amounts of fluid in his glass.

A war movie was playing. However, it was a film featuring humans, and not a representative of this particular race.

A commentator's narration was added to the footage. "How can this be a promised species foretold by the so called ancient Zinj priests? The signals they beam out to space betray the behavior of a violent and conquering breed. When we first began to receive voice transmissions almost twenty years ago, the Royal counsel finally implemented its first sanction against the Zinj religion of "Anameno", or waiting for the manifestation of God through the "Earthman". It confirmed the wisdom of the decisions to enslave the Zinj two centuries ago, so that they would be taught to serve the preservation of our heritage, instead of investing their time and energy in this false hope of the Earthmen bringing the knowledge of their God to us."

The apartment door opened. A female of this species entered with a huge, hairy beast trailing her. She was in a simple dress, and had much longer hair than her counterpart. The "v" shaped bangs, however, appeared to be the same, and so was the black color of her hair. She simply snapped her fingers and the brute behind her lumbered into the kitchen. It began to place the groceries in the appropriate cupboards.

"I don't know why you take Manta to the store just to pick up a few things", commented the man.

"Did you need him here to help you change the channels, dear?" she asked.

All of a sudden, the television flickered into a very bright snow.

"We lost the signal! Blasted satellite! Manta! Come here and adjust the directional dish!" The servant lumbered forward.

"Master Tolem, the signal will come back"

"I want my reception now!" the man shrieked. "I don't care if you have to climb up on the roof!"

"Yes master Tolem", said the gentle giant. Up the stairs Manta went, where he opened up a hatch to reveal the dome shaped roof. Two "moons" shone brightly. One very large heavenly body had clear shadowy shapes of mountains, and valleys as-well-as one side painted an ocean blue. There were small outlines of many habitable structures evident. The other seemed to be much more distant: a cloudy orb with two thin rings at an angle. The stars were partially visible, but a thick, magenta blanket seemed to wrap wispy folds over a good portion of the night sky.

Alone with the majestic celestial panorama before him, Manta seemed to pause to drink the in beauty. He looked out onto the horizon. It was a desert wasteland with mountains and craters before him.

"Manta" yelled the voice below, "what are you waiting for?" He began to rotate the dish ever so slightly, waiting for verbal confirmation of a successful re-alignment.

A loud snap shook the domed building, throwing Manta backward. As he started to slide down the side, he grasped the exhaust stack and clung for life. The satellite dish seemed to become enveloped in an eerie glow as it received a light ray that was being beamed in from above. He managed to pull himself up in time to see the light reflected from the dish to a space atop the dome several feet away. Then there was a violent flash.

Blinded by this unexpected event, Manta struggled to gain a stable foothold on the dome.

"That's great, Manta!" shouted Tolem. "I don't know what you did, but the reception is better than ever!"

* * *

"Where are we, Professor Hawks?" asked Collins.

Jeremiah Hawks surveyed the terrain, then the night sky above.

"We're not in Kansas, Ted; or in western New York. I think we can rule out, the US, and the Virgin Islands for that matter."

"I don't recognize the sky, Professor Hawks."

"I think that eliminates Earth, too."

"Tweed was right! The laser shot has sent us to..."

The teacher pointed to the magenta clouds evident about the star-scape. "I think we are in the Crab Nebula!"

"Wow! I guess we did make history."

"Well, I wouldn't celebrate quite yet. I am not sure if we are around a group of beings who will have then same sense of appreciation for moment as you do."

The two men jumped as they heard something clamoring behind them.

Collins squinted trying to pierce the darkness to see what was making the noise. Unfortunately, he came face to face with a large, hairy, and anthropoid creature.

Failing to hide his fear, he squeaked out an unimpressive scream, and fainted. The thing caught him.

Professor Hawks moved forward, courageously, but not in a manner meant to threaten this creature. He desperately searched for the right words to say that would guarantee Collin's freedom while establishing a first and positive contact.

He didn't have to worry. The creature spoke first.

"You're Earthman!" he pointed.

Jeremiah Hawks thought about his answer carefully. "I am from Earth in the Milky Way galaxy", stated the professor. "I am not sure if I am a particular "Earthman", but I am from that planet."

"I am Manta. I am Zinj!"

Jeremiah Hawks was puzzled. To his amazement, the inhabitant of this planet spoke English. Even more amazing was the fact that he recognized and Collins and himself as inhabitants of Earth.

"Then I greet you, Manta Zinj. I am Professor Hawks. The man you are holding, who was frightened by your sudden appearance, is Ted Collins."

"Tedcollins", Manta repeated. "Professor, it is not safe for you here. If my master sees you, we could be interred."

"Manta" shouted the voice from below once again, "what are you doing? The reception's perfect, now get down here and get our snacks ready!"

"You are a slave!" observed the scientist.

"It matters not, now that you are here. I must get you to the elders. Wait up here. I will come for you after Master Tolem and his mistress are asleep."

The Zinj placed Ted Collins at Jeremiah Hawks' feet. Then he moved to go below. Professor Hawks grasped the giant's arm.

"Where are we?"

"Luna One. It's terra-formed. Below is planet Wakuhn. Above is Luna Two."

"Manta! What are you doing up there! Having a party? I hope you're not tinkling off the dome again!"

"I must go. I will come for you later." Manta disappeared below.

* * *

Alarms flashed. Men, or more accurately, Wakuhnians, rushed to grasp weapons from an open lock up. These specimens appeared to be trimmer than Tolem of Luna One. However, every other characteristic was similar, except for the uniforms.

"Security breach on Luna One, sir", barked an officer into a communication terminal. "A powerful laser pierced the planetary defense shield."

"Any damage?" asked the image in a screen. He was decorated more than the junior officer and clearly his superior.

"Not that kind of laser, sir. It was clearly a Pulsatronic emission! It seemed to join with a satellite signal and end at a reception site", he reported.

"That could be a teleportation attempt!" observed one of the other technicians near the terminal.

"Get a strike team down there fast! I will notify General Manchin immediately!" commanded the superior officer.

"Sir, it gets worse!" added the young officer.

"What do you mean?" bellowed the commander. He was clearly inconvenienced by the incident, and became intolerant of the suggestion of more complications.

"The transmission was from Earth, Colonel."

There was a distinct silence.

"Inter all witnesses for questioning. Spare no suspects. Make sure that was not some sort of teleportation that occurred. The last thing we need is rumors about someone coming from Earth. You have your orders, Lieutenant Daria."

The officer rose when the transmission was finished.

"Let's move! Code Red! We have to seal off the sector.

* * *

Tolem and his wife were sound asleep, the "missus" choosing the comfort of her bed. The master of the house was still on the recliner, the remote control firmly clutched in his hand.

Manta led Jeremiah Hawks and a recovered Ted Collins through the house and out into the night.

"Professor", whispered Collins, "this culture does not seem too advanced to me. The guy's just like my dad! He's passed out in front of the television."

"I know Ted. But your father never had a satellite actuated TV, now did he? More technology does not mean that a culture is more advanced. Sometimes if living is easy, no one seems to grow up."

"I see what you mean. If everyone is in this state of complacency, it would leave them very", Ted paused to become thoughtful, "vulnerable."

"They probably are. But I am sure there is someone watching the store. Otherwise our friend Manta would not be in such a hurry to get us out of the house."

"Yes, Professor Hawks", Manta agreed. "Military come soon. Inter Earthmen. The Wakuhnians will keep Word of God from Zinj."

"What are you babbling about?" Ted asked sarcastically.

"Ted, the Zinj seem to be a race of gentle hulks that have been waiting for the revelation of the special one from Earth. They also seem to have been enslaved by the other creatures we saw, the Wha, Wha..."

"Wakuhnians" helped Manta.

"So we are the Earthmen they're waiting for?" Ted asked.

"Not quite" laughed the professor. "I think that they are waiting for Jesus, the Son of God." Manta stopped short and his eyes widened as he grasped Professor Hawks in his arms, and raised him upward.

"You know Him! You know Him!" exclaimed Manta.

It was Ted's turn to laugh, but his was a cruel and cutting one.

"Yeah, tell him Doc. Tell him how you stiffed your family; probably got them killed, just to end up here. I'm sure that will impress everyone involved."

Manta gently placed the academic down. He eyed this Ted Collins with suspicion.

"Not everyone on Earth believes, Manta. And he is right. I did not appreciate my knowledge of Jesus as I should, and I have failed Him. But I do know the Word of God, and will share what I know with your people."

Manta paused to understand Jeremiah Hawks'.

"Let us hurry. I will need to get back to master Tolem's house before they wake."

* * *

Lights glared brightly. Tolem awoke from his perch on his recliner to meet nose to nose with the muzzle of a weapon. His wife screeched as she was dragged out of bed. Soldiers filled the room.

"Where have you been all night!" barked Lieutenant Daria.

"Here! I was watching the television monitor!" His wife shook her head to confirm her husband's assertion.

"Then where is your Zinj?"

"I don't know. Isn't he here? Manta? Manta?" Tolem turned his head to look to the roof. "Manta? Are you up on the dome?"

"Why would your Zinj be up there?" Daria asked as he referred to a scripted note pad, "Naldo Tolem?"

"Our reception fades because of the satellite orbit. I don't have a power direction finder. So we send him up on the roof."

"Yes, yes" nodded his wife. "Sometimes he stays up there too long. He tinkles off the dome, you know. Is that why you are here? Did he tinkle on you or on a neighbor?"

"Tinkle? What is your wife talking about, Tolem?"

"Tinkle, uh, he piddles," she elaborated.

The officer stilled seemed confused. A sergeant came up and whispered in his ear. "Oh, that! No, we are not here because of that. Did anything strange happen when he was up on the roof tonight?"

"Well, the television was really acting up. We saw a flash, and then the reception was better then ever! But Manta didn't come down right away, so we thought he was tinkling.

"That is enough about the tinkling! Did you hear anything? Was he talking to anyone?"

"I thought he was" said the wife, "but who would be on top of the dome with him? He came down alone."

Another soldier climbed down the ladder from the dome.

"Sir, the dish is scorched. That signal definitely reflected from this dish."

"What signal?" Tolem asked.

"Take them into custody!" Mr. and Mrs. Tolem were grabbed by some soldiers and dragged outside of their home into a waiting shuttle.

As the Tolems were taken out, forcibly and with much protest, an odd looking police officer stepped in. He was a large and muscular being, similar to the Zinj in stature, but with a wider, almost reptilian face. His forehead had a boney plate, and other than some tuff of black hair, he was bald.

“Who is in charge, here?” he asked with a gravely voice.

“I am” answered the Lieutenant as he stepped forward. “Who is asking?” replied Daria tersely.

“I am Prefect Calpern, sir, and I was wondering why the DDF is in my precinct, and why I was not notified of your incursion into my jurisdiction.”

“Well, then Prefect Calpern, do your homework next time!” barked the young officer fiercely. “The Domestic Defense Force does not have to notify the local constables when there is a possible first contact with an alien race or a clear breach of Empire security. There was a possible teleportation into this sector, and I am here under due Imperial authority. As you are well aware, we do not possess such teleportation technology, so the prospect of such an incursion into Wakuhnian space must receive our utmost attention!"

"I stand corrected, Lieutenant," stated Calpern meekly. "This is my first assignment, sir," he began to explain.

"Then get me some intelligence on where we can find the Zinj in this sector, and perhaps it will not be your last! You are dismissed!"

The local constable cowered out of the doorway. Daria signaled for his non commissioned officers to gather.

"This *is* ground zero!" he stated through clenched teeth. "Tell the Colonel. We are going to need more troops. I have no doubt that we will have to round up every Zinj in this sector before this business is over!"

*　　　*　　　*

"It was wise that you brought them here, Manta", stated the aged Zinj before them. His fur was very gray, with only specs of dark over him. He walked with a slight gimp and was hunched over as he moved deeper into the cave.

"You cannot return. Your masters have been interred."

"No!" Manta exclaimed in disappointment.

"What difference should that make", asked Collins, "you were being kept as a slave?" The elder Zinj nodded at this question knowingly.

"Yes. Wakuhnians keep us as slaves. But we still love. And serve. It is what the Grand Master would want."

"Who is this Grand Master?" Collins struggled with the Zinj elder's assertion. "What is he talking about, Professor?"

Jeremiah Hawks did not even hear the question. His attention seemed drawn away.

"Professor?" asked Collins.

"What is it, Ted?"

"You don't seem too concerned about the fact that our Zinj benefactor's 'masters' are in the slammer; or the fact that we are being hunted; or the statement our senior citizen just made about some "Grand Master" who wants them to love the people who are oppressing them".

"I am not having a problem with any of this, Ted. It makes perfect sense!"

"Could you please clue me in?" demanded Ted.

"You know the 'Grand Master?" asked the Zinj.

"Yes, he does" testified Manta.

"Are you involved in some cosmic game?" Collins ventured yet another question.

"Ted, this isn't some Twilight Zone plot. They are waiting for us to reveal Jesus to them. He is their 'Grand Master'. He's the one teaching them to love their enemies."

"Professor is correct" stated Manta. Their walk brought the two into a large underground room. In the center of the room was a pedestal, and on it was a book.

"We are here. It is time for assembly. I am elder Joktar. We will have council to see if you are the promised Earthman."

"Joktar, there is no need to go on with the assembly. Neither of us are the promised Earthman."

"Speak for yourself, Professor. I don't want to be given up to these Wakuhnians. It may be worth a shot trying to fulfill a couple of promises, just to get a chance to get back to Earth".

Both Zinj seemed to ignore Ted Collins. In fact, even Jeremiah Hawks seemed to ignore Ted Collins.

"What's with you, Professor? Your attention is on something else."

"Ted, don't you feel...?" the scientist began. Somehow he knew the answer.

"What are you babbling about? All I feel is scared as well as a certain measure of contempt for this culture, and these sorry creatures."

"Well Ted, look around. There are certainly a lot of sorry creatures with us!"

The graduate student glanced upward and sideways. The walls of this cavern were filled to capacity with Zinj. About ten thousand or so was Ted's estimate. Along the walls seats and steps were carved out, and each seat had an occupant. Some were even standing.

"We're in trouble, Professor."

"I don't think so. However, I am not so sure about you, Ted. I think you better let me do the talking. I wouldn't try to inspire an armed rebellion either. I am sure that there may be a Zinj or two who would take offense or turn us in."

"They may turn us in, any way!"

"I hope so, for their sakes! In fact, I will suggest it"

"Are you nuts, Professor?"

"Ted, these creatures do not have access to the technology we require to make our way back home. I am not sure if the Wakuhnian's do either. In any event, I am not going to ask the Zinj to risk themselves on our behalf."

"You're right" Collins agreed. These creatures are in no position to help us get back home."

Joktar slowly walked into the center of the huge recess. He raised his hands upward. The gathering grew very quiet.

"We have the Earthmen," he said with a loud voice. "Manta brought them. One knows the 'Grand Master' and one does not. He is not the promised one, but he knows Him. We will hear from him, and then decide we must".

Joktar motioned for the professor. Jeremiah Hawks moved to the pedestal.

"Joktar?" he whispered. "May I look at your sacred text?" Joktar did not answer, but raised his hands once again.

"The one called Jeremiah Hawks has asked to consult the written oracle!"

There was a loud murmur. The kind of grumbling you would expect from 10,000 startled gorillas.

Jeremiah Hawks read with amazement. At first, he was hoping that at center stage was a copy of the Bible. Though there were some selected passages, the oracle was an accounting of Zinj history.

From the beginning the planet Wakuhn had two distinct races. The Zinj were dedicated toward technology at first. They reached for the stars and sent out a one way mission. It landed on Earth centuries ago and managed to teleport back this oracle. The writings changed the hearts and minds of the Zinj as a people. They became dedicated to waiting for the promise of the "Earthman", who would unlock the Word of God for them.

While they waited, they gave themselves over to benevolence. In time, the planet Wakuhn's other race had developed an ambitious attitude. They supplanted the Zinj's peaceful intentions, and they enslaved them. Still, this converted race endured persecution while hoping for the promised "Earthman". They became devoted to the proverb remitted to them from Earth: 'It is more blessed to give than receive."

Jeremiah Hawks was astounded! With only precious few verses from the scriptures, their whole culture was transformed. As he read, he saw that it was the Zinj who motivated the establishment of English as the common language, so the oracle and scriptures could be better understood. The streaming transmissions from Earth seemed to inspire the inhabitants of Wakuhn to be contemporary with the language.

The academic stood in awe of the Zinj's hunger for God's Word and obedient attitude! He was ashamed of his own selfishness. He felt so unworthy.

Finally, he turned to the end of the oracle. To his surprise, instead of more pages of text, he found what seemed to be a lock box. He became even more astonished as the keyhole seemed very familiar. Almost in disbelief, he fitted his office key, a "skeleton" circa 1935, and inserted it into the lock.

He began to turn the lock. A distinct "click" resonated throughout the cavern. Ten thousand Zinj kept a silent vigil. Jeremiah Hawks opened the lock box to reveal a King James Bible. It was printed in the original seventeenth century English. He reverently raised it above his head. As he did so, the assembly erupted into spontaneous celebration!

Ted Collins found the uproar unnerving. The significance of the moment was lost on him. The Zinj faithful continued their celebration until Joktar raised his hands and encouraged them to resume their reverent hush.

"The Earthman has fulfilled the prophecy! The Word of God has been unlocked for us!" Jeremiah Hawks placed the Bible back into the box. While he may have physically granted access to the Bible's content, unlocking its meaning for the Zinj had only just begun. With 1611 English, there would literally be some translation to do! The professor wondered why God chose him to fulfill this promise, and not someone more theologically inclined. Before he could speak, a loud voice pierced the silence.

"There are troopers at the entrance!"

Suddenly Zinj scattered in all directions. Manta grasped a disappointed Jeremiah Hawks and a startled Ted Collins. The elder removed the oracle from its place on the pedestal. Manta and Joktar led the two deeper in to the cave. They ran. In the distance they heard the blasts of weapons and the screams of the unfortunate targets. They arrived at a small space dock carved out of the rocks. The scientist and his graduate student were plunked onto a vehicle and then belted in.

"This will take you to the Outerworlds. You can hide there", said Manta.

"Guard this" stated Joktar. He handed Jeremiah Hawks the oracle. "Tell us what is needed to fulfill it. Keep it safe."

"I will" promised the professor. "Who will we meet when we get there?"

"A guardian will meet you. Now go!"

The weapons fire sounded closer. Manta closed the hatch. Jeremiah Hawks turned to see Manta and Joktar face the attackers. Both fell as ray blasts hit each one. But before a gun could be trained on them, their craft was off in an instant.

It sped around corners and accelerated through a long tubular tunnel. Just as quickly, the two were propelled out into space. The craft raced even further when with a blinding flash, even the stars themselves seemed to rocket past them.

* * *

The lumbering freighter appeared more like a puffer fish then an interstellar craft. Whether an act of genius or not, it provided this space ship a certain measure of safety from the frequent acts of piracy in this sector of space. In its pilot's chair rested what appeared to be a very skinny person. A closer examination revealed a rather worm like creature-well it was a worm! Its head was barely thicker than its neck, and other than the fact that it had arms, a leather flight jacket and something reminiscent of an aviator's cap, its segmented torso was that of a grub.

"Vermis!" a voice yelled from outside of the command bridge. "Have you been snitching the hydraulic oil?"

Vermis' eyes narrowed and lips smacked as he recollected the satisfaction if his appetite. Then he returned from his tour of memory lane to fabricate a lie.

"Why would I do that?" he said with a peculiar accent. "I know that we need it for the collectors.

A rotund but much shorter creature waddled into the bridge. His features seemed to betray a hoggish heritage. He waived a three-fingered hand.

"Don't worry! I've got plenty! I brought extra. Your species thrives on hydrocarbons on your planet! I guess having highly refined product is like eating a frosted dessert."

"More like a shake, Captain Boaracious."

The porcine officer patiently worked at a secondary station, humming as he examined a flight plan. He too was arrayed in a flight jacket, but instead of an aviator's headdress, he sported a ball cap with a dwarfed bill.

"I'm glad you didn't take any", he began. "I couldn't obtain any hydrocarbon lubricants, so I had to settle for a synthetic on Dino Prime.

Vermis' normal gray color began to pail white as saliva dripped from his mouth.

"And you know how synthetics make you sick," Boaracious continued.

Vermis, the worm, suddenly jumped from his seat. He half hopped, half ran out of the bridge, his artificial left leg thumping on the metal deck as he left. A young woman crossed his path as she entered the bridge. Red hair poured bountifully from the sides of her head, but that was it. Her orange skin was filled with flaking scales which began on her forehead and continued to the top of her scalp. Her bright red eyes glistened even in the poorly lit shadows of the command bridge.

"Camille, please take the pilot's chair", instructed Boaracious.

"Yes sir." She settled in. "Vermis drank synthetic again, eh sir?"

"Is the Nebula filled with ions? I've heard of a drinking problem, but he does carry it a bit too far."

A youthful Wakuhnian entered the bridge. "Hey flame-babe", he said to the new pilot.

"The name is Camille. Just because you are a blue blood, doesn't give you the right to talk down to me!"

"Ease up, sister! I'm a blue blood hauling trash beyond the Outerworlds. Don't link me with my wretched race! Judge me by my politics! I'd rather be a slave than beat a slave."

"Enough of the lectures today, Elvis, the captain addressed the Wakuhnian. He was aptly named. He wore the characteristic 'V' hair line draped to the side in a wave. The bridge officer continued. "Vermis drank some of the hydraulic fluid again, so I would appreciate it if you could do a quick inventory for me in the hold."

"Sure boss. I guess that's why he curled up over the head regurgitating his little worm guts out. I'll be back in a jiff, flame-babe!"

"He's sooo annoying!" Camille protested.

"Only because he likes you" Commander Boaracious teased. "Imagine! A Wakuhnian and a "Flameboyant"! Just think of the saving on the heating bills during the winter!"

"My planet may be near the hot fringes of the Nebula, but it is sure better than being a transplanted Porker, sir!"

"True, Camille. Let's face facts. We are just a troop of misfits! Each of us abandoned the planet of our birth because we do not agree with the way they run their society. I guess picking up the garbage of the Nebula suits us all better than living the lies our cultures feed us."

"Sir how is it we can all agree about what the truth is not, but we can't agree what the truth is?"

"Because Red", said the tusker sagaciously, "we haven't found the all important "Debris of Truth"."

Vermis hobbled back onto the bridge. "I'm okay now, sir."

"I need some fuel calculations. Let's work on them, for now. We'll let Red drive for a while."

"Yes, sir."

"What is the "Debris of Truth"?" asked Camille.

"That is simple, Red. If truth has been discarded by a culture, it is sure to pile up somewhere. Since truth is true, it cannot disappear. If it has been discarded, it has to be left somewhere."

"And some day we will find the right garbage heap!" stated the Flameboyant helmsperson.

"That's right. One of these days we will discover the "Debris of Truth"

Instantly the spacecraft rocked as a flash of light streaked past. "Yikes!" exclaimed the captain.

"We were almost vaporized by a ship dropping out of light speed!" exclaimed Vermis.

"What was that?" Boaracious asked. "What was that?" he repeated.

"I have it on the scope, sir" stated Camille. "It looks like a Zinj mining shuttle.

"With warp drive?" asked the commander. He pressed a button on a nearby console. "Elvis, you Zinj loving hooligan, get up here! We need you!"

"Yes boss!" was the answer over the radio.

"How can that be a Zinj mining shuttle? Let's turn this bucket around and see if it needs help. If it is in good shape, I'm sure we can sell it for a good price."

"But sir, what about the pilot and passengers?' asked Camille?

"Red, if pirates get them, they will all be killed. At least I'll give them safe passage to Skyport Seven. Their ship will probably come close to the cost of safe transport."

"A Zinj mining shuttle out here?' sighed Vermis. "It sounds like a set up to me, sir. I think we should pass on this."

"You're a worm, Vermis. You think we should pass on everything!"

"Coming about to their starboard, Captain", informed Camille. "We should be able to get a look at their ugly, hairy faces through the cockpit window."

Elvis entered the bridge.

"You are just in. time. Some of your Zinj friends just dropped out of warp and almost roasted our tail! As unlikely as it seems, they may be escaping slaves! I would appreciate it if you would talk with them."

"Sure boss."

All eyes searched through the blackness anticipating a lit cockpit to reveal the pilot and passengers as Zinj. What they saw surprised them all; that is all but Elvis; he shook visibly.

"What's wrong, son?" asked Boaracious.

"Earthmen!" exclaimed Elvis.

There was a moment of silence as each being tried to comprehend the gravity of the moment.

"Captain" began Camille, "I think we may have found our 'Debris of Truth'!"

Chapter Three: The Debris of Truth

The fuel spent shuttle was a drift in space. The teacher and his student studied the alien controls in an attempt to determine the craft's operational condition. Ted turned around to gaze behind their transport. He became alarmed.

"Professor Hawks! Do you see that?" exclaimed Ted Collins.

"Yes, it is another ship."

"Let's get going! It's gaining on us!"

"We're stopped, Ted. I am afraid that this vehicle has gone as far as it is intended to go. Besides, this may be a pre-arranged rendezvous."

The scientist and Ted were helpless as the strange looking craft approached. Like a jaw, the lower front of the ship slowly opened as it drew near. Once the smaller shuttle was inside, it was shut, trapping the two earthmen.

"Where are we, Professor?"

"It looks like we're in the belly of a whale."

"That is not funny, Professor Hawks. I'm no Jonah, though."

"That is a pity, Ted. It took Jonah three days in the whale's stomach before he cried out to God. I wonder how many days in this situation before you do?"

"Give it a rest, Professor. If I didn't feel threatened every moment, I think I would be enjoying this experience."

"Like I said; it is a pity. I don't feel threatened at all. In spite of all my failures, I know God has been taking care of us. He has plans for us out here.

"Well, Professor, I like making my own plans."

There was a momentary strained silence. The scientist brought their focus back to the business at hand.

"If I can trust my meager piloting skills, I believe that this indicator is telling us that we are in a pressurized environment. We should be able to open the cockpit, and at least go outside of our vehicle to meet our hosts."

"Try that button, Professor," encouraged Ted. The cockpit lifted up over the earthmen's heads. They both stepped out into the cavernous, dark holding area.

"Peeew!" protested Ted. "What is that smell?"

"Trash! It would seem that we ended up in a pile of trash."

A deep metallic echo sounded. Jeremiah Hawks looked around to see a hatch door begin to open.

"Over there", he pointed. "Let's go", said Jeremiah Hawks. He was still clutching the oracle underneath his left arm. The door swung open.

"Why me?" protested Vermis. "Why do I have to go first?"

"You're expendable, that's why" said Elvis.

"The word is expandable. And I will give you a full report."

"I will be glad to help you with that report" offered Professor Hawks. He extended his hand to the unique life-form before him. I am Jeremiah Hawks from Earth. This is my assistant, Ted Collins

The worm shook the professor's hand, then Ted's. Elvis disappeared down the dark corridor.

"My name is Vermis. I am the pilot of this garbage scow, the Commodities III."

Ted struggled to remove the sticky secretion left after the handshake.

"Were you expecting us?" asked the academic as the two stepped from the holding area. Ted followed at a distance.

"Not really. You dropped out of warp and almost onto our heads. What was your flight path?"

"I'm not really sure, Vermis. We began at Luna One. The Zinj sent us off. I guess the Wakuhnians are wary of earthmen." They walked along a hallway. Ted grabbed at his teacher's free hand to get his attention, only to get another handful of slime.

"Professor Hawks, you're speaking to a worm!"

"Ted there is no need to state the obvious."

"I'm not offended" Vermis said. "I get a lot of abuse around here. Why did the Zinj send you away in such a hurry?"

"We were being hidden. Then the police found us."

Elvis appeared from behind and pointed at the oracle.

"Oh, and I suppose they gave this to you for safe keeping?"

"Who are you?" demanded Ted.

"Obviously, he is a Wakuhnian, Ted. Maybe he is one with a conscience."

"And a terrible hair," added the lab assistant.

"Just move along so you can meet the Captain" said Elvis. The metal deck hallway opened to the bridge.

"Look what we have here," Boaracious stated. "two earthmen? Indeed!"

Vermis stepped forward to introduce them. "This is Professor Jeremiah Hawks of Earth and his assistant Ted Collins."

"I'm Captain Horatio Boaracious of the Interplanetary Reclamation Corporation. Under interplanetary law it is my prerogative to impound your craft, but that same law directs me to conduct you safely to the nearest port of call."

"That's acceptable to us," stated the academic. "I would prefer a neutral port, a haven safe; from Wakuhnian jurisdiction.

"I will agree to your request. And what is that you have there?"

"It's the Zinj oracle" Elvis stated.

"It is a copy? You are studying the text for the Zinj?" Boaracious asked.

"No. It's the real item. I can tell by the embroidery on the cover."

Boaracious moved closer to the scientist from Earth and eyed him suspiciously. "What devious plan are you up to, sir?"

"None, Captain. My assistant and I were teleported against our will to this sector of space. The Zinj befriended us while the Wakuhnian police have been hunting us. These oracles were entrusted to my care and we were sent away in the vehicle you have recovered. I have no idea of where we were going, only that we would meet a 'guardian'."

"Woe!" exclaimed Elvis. "Boss this is heavy duty!"

"Hmmm," said Boaracious thoughtfully. "The story does seem quite reasonable. Have you had anything to eat?"

"Not in a day and a half," Ted volunteered.

"Vermis please take our guests to the galley and get them some grub"

"Captain?" protested Vermis.

"I apologize for my figure of speech! Feed them and, please, not some of your regurgitated slop!"

Ted cringed at the thought of eating pre-digested food.

"Yes sir!" Vermis placed a guiding hand on Ted's shoulder, leaving a wad of slime behind. Professor Hawks followed. Once they cleared the bridge, Elvis moved to confront his captain.

"So, what are you going to do? These guys are hot! I am sure a Wakuhnian patrol frigate will be scouring the area for them."

"I am not sure. Let's scuttle the Zinj mining craft at the end of the warp trail. Try to mimic a warp chamber explosion."

"We should not go back", cautioned Camille. She was listening in as she piloted the craft.

"What then?" Elvis queried.

. "We will let it drift, cockpit open. Pirates will pick it up."

"Good idea, Red."

"So, we're going to protect them?"

"No we are going to protect our investment," started Boaracious. "I believe that the oracle will fetch a fair price from the Zinj. I do want to learn more about our passengers. Meanwhile, set a course for Skyport Seven of the Outerworlds, so at least we are out of Wakuhnian jurisdiction."

Meanwhile, Vermis had led his guest's into the galley.

"What happened to your leg?" asked Ted.

"Nothing" stated Vermis.

"I don't understand?"

"One 'leg' is his tail, Ted. The artificial limb is intended to give him the appearance of being a biped."

"That's correct, Professor Hawks. You can't get a good job in this sector of space if you slither around."

"Are your arms, artificial?" asked Ted.

"No, they are real. Actually, you only see the top two." Abruptly, six more limbs appeared through Vermis' leather vest, three on each side.

"The hands are artificial", he stated. "You can't get a good job in this sector if you just have setae".

At that moment, the entire space craft was rocked. Vermis, Ted Collins and Jeremiah Hawks, were all thrown from their chairs. Their food splattered all over the galley, with a tray landing on Ted's head. As he grasped the tray, his groaned as more sticky slime from Vermis was transferred from the tray to his hand. Disgusted, he turned to the worm.

"What's going on?" protested Ted.

His question was never answered. The lights went out and an eerie silence ensued. Many long minutes later, the lights came back on.

"What happened?" asked Jeremiah Hawks

"We've been boarded by pirates", informed Vermis.

"Now we're in for it!" exclaimed Ted

"Not really. It happens all the time! Usually they wait until we are in their sector, though."

"Get everyone up here" shouted Boaracious over the intercom.

"Let's go and meet Jock LaFeet!"

"Just when you thought it couldn't get any worse..." complained Ted.

Vermis led the Earthmen back onto the bridge. There an four legged creature grimaced as he threatened with a pistol of sorts, in one hand, and a crab like claw in another.

"LaFeet, I presume" said Ted Collins.

"I'm LaFeet!" roared a voice by the pilot's seat. Ted and Jeremiah Hawks turned to view the pirate captain.

He, indeed, lived up to his name. While dwarfish and with a patch over his left eye, LaFeet did have very large feet.

"I should have guessed", Ted said sarcastically. "The nightmare continues"

"So", LaFeet began, "these are the earth creatures Horatio spoke about? Not as fearsome as I expected."

"They have been very quiet during their stay" volunteered Captain Boaracious.

"They haven't even eaten much" stated Vermis.

"The resident worm on the garbage scow speaks!" exclaimed LaFeet. "Okay, Boaracious, what are you and your crew up to? I'll bet these aliens are more valuable than you're lettin' on!"

There was a hushed silence. It was broken by Ted Collins. "Not valuable, just politically desirable."

"What do you mean?" asked the pirate.

"You know what I mean, Captain," began Ted as he moved to LaFeet's side. "I have only been in this system a couple of days, and it is very clear that half of the beings I have encountered have feared us as some sort of gods, and the other half have been after our hide. Seems to me, if a pirate captain had an "earther" as a first mate, it would certainly be a boost to his prestige. It may make boarding easier, and take some fight out of your enemies. "

LaFeet scratched his chin and looked up at the much taller earthman. "I like you're thinking! But why would you want to leave this crew? What about your friend here?"

"It's his fault that I am in this mess away from my home. He is more interested in that Zinj Oracle under his arm than pursuing any good business opportunities."

"LaFeet stepped back in terror.

"The Zinj Oracle!" he exclaimed. LaFeet cast a fearful glance at Boaracious, Elvis, Vermis and finally at Camille.

"You're playing a dangerous game, Horatio! But I won't play! Me and my crew will be leaving, and quickly at that!"

Ted stood before LaFeet.

"And my offer of service?" he asked.

"I gladly accept it. You may come along. After a brief training period, I will make you my first mate! But you don't have time to pack, because we are leaving now."

"Ted" protested Jeremiah Hawks. "We should not separate!"

"Professor, you are more intent upon being God's messenger to these creatures. Frankly, I could care less. If I can't make it back home, I am going to obtain every advantage I can to live here!"

Ted Collins followed the hurried procession off the bridge.

The scientist moved toward Horatio to speak, but with an upraised hand, Captain Boaracious urged him to silence. The lights flickered. The garbage scow lurched.

"They're gone" announced Camille. "He warped right out of the sector!"

Quite unexpectedly, everyone on the bridge, except for the professor, threw their head back and laughed wildly.

"What is so funny?" asked Jeremiah Hawks.

"LaFeet!" roared Boaracious! "I know that we are just a garbage scow, but your fellow earthling just signed up with the most incompetent pirate in the whole galaxy!"

Vermis draped a slimy arm over the academic's shoulder as he laughed.

"One out of every two earth people must be an utter moron!" he said.

"And to think" Camille piped in, "I was beginning to think he was cute!"

"There you go!" said Boaracious, "Camille always dates a loser!"

In spite of his concern for Ted Collins, the scientist from Earth could not help but begin to smile at this display of mirth.

"He's that bad?"

"He's worse than bad. Once he purchased a hijacked freighter of bullion."

"Mushroom bullion!" laughed Elvis. "Once he misread a stolen ships manifest. He thought it said "computers"

“It was compost!" stated Vermis! "He paid ten times what it was actually worth to get rid of it! He ended up dumping it on my planet just to unload it. Boy did he take a bath because of that bad deal!"

"Everyone who visits your planet has to take a bath!" teased Horatio Boaracious.

"Captain!" screamed Camille. "Something's coming up fast! It is on a collision course!"

Suddenly, all of the crew took a station on the bridge and were deathly serious. The professor looked on and prayed.

"What is it?" he asked.

"I don’t know! I don’t know!” exclaimed Vermis. It is coming up on us fast. It's not a missile! It looks like a comet, or a meteor."

"Take evasive action!" commanded Boaracious.

Camille called for all of the impulse power available as the cumbersome craft propelled forward. She then executed a portside turn. The projectile seemed to overshoot them, but quickly corrected and tracked them once again.

"It's following us! It's following us!' informed Camille. “Is it a missile?”

"Ten seconds to impact!" called out Elvis.

"Earthman, do something!" yelled Horatio Boaracious.

Jeremiah Hawks glanced at the Oracle in his hands. It began to glow.

“This must be the guardian,” he declared. "Bring us to a full stop, Captain Boaracious. I believe that this is my rendezvous."

"We may as well," said Elvis. "We can't out run it."

Horatio Boaracious nodded his assent. The spacecraft slowed to a halt.

The oracle continued to glow. The garbage scow's lights flickered once again.

"Something has entered the ship through the collector."

Once again Boaracious nodded. He moved to a small locker and pulled out a pistol.

"You won't need that" said Jeremiah Hawks.

The bridge door opened. A tall, sculpted figure stepped inside to look toward the professor. It was about six foot five with a golden frame and midnight blue trunks. An image of a burning candle was on its chest.

"The Oracle!" exclaimed the intruder in an electronic voice. Then he collapsed.

"What is he?" asked Camille.

Elvis and the Jeremiah rushed to the creature's side. "He is a construct of some kind, a robot?"

"A Guardian!" said Elvis in awe.

"What are you talking about?'" asked Horatio.

"The Zinj speak about a special sentinel. Its job, according to legend is to retrieve the Oracle if it is ever taken."

"Whatever its role, it is a robot" observed the professor. "But I am convinced that it was sent to meet with me."

Elvis rose from the robot's side.

"It's a Guardian. And you are now the 'Keeper of the Oracle'. Unfortunately, your Guardian is not up to its task or protecting it."

"Where did it come from?" asked Horatio. "Vermis, can you get any sensor readings?"

"I am checking the telemetry. My best guess is-THE PULSAR!"

"That's not possible!" exclaimed Boaracious.

"The pulsar at the center of the Nebula?" asked the professor rhetorically. He moved to Vermis' station. Please show me how to use this equipment, Vermis.

"What are you looking for?"

"I want to see if the Guardian is emitting Nultron energy. This would be the same kind of energy that brought me to this sector of space."

"What kind of energy is that?" asked Elvis.

"Here! It's the same wave signature. What do you call this energy?"

"Pulsatronic" stated Elvis.

"And all of the planet Wakuhn and its moons use it?"

"It is used primarily for communication equipment Professor Hawks."

"Can you direct a sensor at our visitor?"

"I'm way ahead of your, Earthman" said Elvis as he pointed a device at the fallen Guardian. "Wow. I can't figure this out."

"Let me try". Elvis handed the instrument over to Jeremiah Hawks.

"Well" began Boaracious impatiently, "what is it?"

"Our friend here is a construct that has been carved out of the core of a pulsar or made in a similar fashion. Somehow the material was drawn out, with his design and pattern. The best I can tell, he is in a dormant state, totally drained of usable energy."

"Perhaps he is too far away from the pulsar. I would guess he is designed to draw energy from it," speculated Vermis.

"You're awful bright for a worm! But he is not too far from the pulsar. I just think he overextended himself getting to us. Likewise, the hull of the ship will insulate him from the pulsar's energy that is saturating this sector. If it didn't we would be dead right now. I bet that there is a way to recharge him."

"But how?" asked Elvis.

"Simple" interjected Horatio. "I bet that the answer is in the Oracle."

"He needs more than a recharging" spoke Camille. Her hand was placed upon the construct's chest.

"What do you mean?' asked Elvis.

"He does not have a heart!"

"He wouldn't," stated the professor. "He's a robot!"

"Not that kind of heart. Did you see his eyes? They were blank and without life. I have heard the legend of the Guardian. Guardians are supposed to have a heart for their mission. They are supposed to be special."

"How does a robot get a heart?" asked Vermis.

There was a momentary pause in the conversation.

"Captain", began Jeremiah Hawks, "Horatio. I need time to study the Oracle and our friend here. I know that you and your crew did not ask for me, or for this adventure, or to get involved in a cosmic struggle. I have been sent into this sector by God, not just to bring this Oracle to understanding, but to add what I know of the Word of God. There are many, like Ted Collins, on my planets that have rejected God's Son, Jesus Christ, and His plan for their life. And just like him, they are up to a lot of mischief and actively oppose God's plans."

"What makes you think we didn't ask for this?" said Camille. "Jeremiah Hawks, we are all misfits and rejects on this vessel. Each of us turned our backs on our self-serving cultures. Deep inside we knew that there is something better, but we just didn't know what."

Everyone in the room nodded in agreement with the redhead's words.

"Tell us the Word of God that you know", Boaracious pleaded. "I don't know if we can smell the truth, but we certainly know what trash smells like!"

All eyes were on Jeremiah Hawks. It was a time to come up with the right words for beings desperate for the knowledge of God. Where should he start? Somehow he knew.

"God so loved the world that He gave his only begotten Son, that whoever believes on Him shall not perish but have eternal life."

There was a pause as each considered the academic's words.

"You mean, forever?" asked Vermis. "You mean that there is hope for us?"

"God's desire is for us to know Him. But in order to know Him we must repent of our desire to rule our own lives and from the destructive behavior that result from the rejection of God's authority."

Horatio Boaracious looked at his crew. Camille, Vermis and Elvis nodded their assent. He spoke, but not simply for himself.

"What must we do to be saved, Professor Hawks?"

Chapter Four: The Striker Pilot

The sleek narrow craft whisked along the starlit background, barely noticeable even to the trained eye. The arrow shape and rounded lines framed a masterful design. Combined with the charred black hull it could easily make any starship ensign question the verity of his sensor readings. But a starship ensign was not tracking this wraith-like craft. Instead, this vessel was being tracked in an uninhabited sector of deep space.

A cockpit tapered from the expansive tail fin. Inside a petite but powerful fighter, a shadowy cobalt helmet hid the features of the person within. The pilot was arrayed in this dark armor and the astronaut seemed molded into his flight chair. Infrared band instrumentation permitted privacy where even the faintest hint of light could betray concealment. A Striker pilot was on the hunt today. Its sensors were locked on this foreign vessel.

"A blockade runner?" he mused. "I wonder, 'Who are you?' and 'Who are you supplying?'"

His own craft followed at a judicious distance. A dangerous game was about to ensue. If the Striker had been detected, he would undoubtedly be led into a trap. If not, this bold investigator could still be outnumbered in his attempt to uphold the law. However, being outnumbered was not new.

"Let's hope he mistakes me for an ion shadow, Ian."

"Hope?" whispered a voice, calling in question the use of the term. The utterance emanated from a speaker on the crafts control panel.

"Hope, Ian. I know that it is not a part of your strategic computations. Since you are my newly installed Holographic Officer for Weapons, Navigation, and Data analysis you are going to have to learn about a pilot's intuitive observations. Hope is a desire to trust that what I am doing is right and just, and that by doing my duty the advantage will work in my favor. I hope my instincts are correct in assuming that our blockade runner has not detected us."

"I have kept our distance and speed exact enough for his sensors to conclude that we are simply his ion engine's displacement. The odds are..."

"The odds are, Ian, that our friend has rather refined instincts, too."

"Sentient beings-you are so emotional."

"And we are so unpredictable. According to the book, I should close in now, and destroy our independent operator. The problem is that I don't recognize the configuration of his craft. Even the energy signature is unique. You're right about emotions! I have a bad feeling about this!"

"It could be converted Dino barge or an Outerworld satellite shuttle. The energy signature, however, does not match any know Nebular region vessel."

"Tell me something I don't know, Ian. I would like to find out if the relatively modest speed is intended as a stealth tactic, or if this craft is on a deliberate course and the crew is oblivious of any breach of Wakuhnian space or trade statutes. I am wondering if the pilot is new to the region and unaware of us altogether."

"Auto pilot," announced Ian. "I detect a faint electromagnetic pulse."

"Asleep at the wheel, or just a clever ploy?" the pilot mused.

"Perhaps the crew has been incapacitated by illness," suggested Ian.

"That is a possibility. It is also possible it was attacked by pirates, however, the craft would have been commandeered." The Striker pilot was quiet and speculative.

"It is time to move in. I'll take the stick. Calculate the best possible target points for the blasters and arm a torpedo in case we have to slam her good."

The fighter careened into action, its broad, sail like wings slicing through the obscurity of endless night. The side wings were set well in the aft of this space vehicle. Another sail like tail began just behind the cockpit and broadened to the very back of the ship. Menacing guns were mounted at the furthermost reaches of the wings.

As the Striker pilot closed the distance, he marveled at the absence of any response by the blockade-runner.

"Open a communication channel, Ian. Use translation protocols.

"This is Striker 117. You have breached Wakuhnian Space with an unlicensed craft. I can only assume that you have contraband on board. Please respond."

There was no reply, not even the crackle of static or the hint of the engagement of a communicator.

"This is Striker 117 to Luna Two base. I have a drifter in sector 9117276. No response or any positive ID. I will attempt to disable its remaining engine drive. I will require a tug to conduct our drifter to a designated port of call for containment, decontamination and inspection."

"Striker 117, we will dispatch two tugs and an Elite Class Cruiser, The Protector of the Realm. Mark the course with a beacon. Disable the vessel. Secure the area. Guard the craft until your escort arrives. The estimated time of arrival is fourteen hours."

"I have your instructions. I am engaging the tracking beacon. I will disable the vessel and await the escorts."

The guns streaked multiple bursts that staggered the mysterious craft. Ian's target points seemed to be accurate. The ship's momentum began to slow and its ion signature wane. Soon it was adrift, almost totally still.

"Fourteen hour countdown has commenced. Here's where we get to watch and wait, Ian. It almost makes a guy hope some pirates come by just to ease the boredom."

"There is that word, hope once again." Ian stated. "Do your instincts detect pirate activity my sensors do not?"

"No Ian. Still, it does not make sense that no one else is aware of this vessel. Let's begin a visual sweep of the sector. You're sensors and my eyes. We will fly circular routes around this space craft and broaden the diameter each rotation."

"I have some indication of debris in sector 9117279. Our charts seem to show several asteroids. "

"Great. Where there are asteroids, there are pirates taking advantage of the cover. Perhaps our vessel was intending a rendezvous there."

The Striker flew the search pattern. Each circumlocution merely confirmed the loneliness of this parsec. As far as the pilot was concerned, the area was secure.

"That killed two hours, Ian. I wonder if there is anything else exciting to do?"

"We can extrapolate our fuel consumption", Ian suggested.

"Oh, I bet that would be interesting! Let's first get adjacent to the vessel and try to pick up any bioelectric readings. I still want to know if there is anything living on board."

The craft inched closer to the disabled vessel. Ian's readings were inconclusive.

"What's the problem, Ian? We should be reading something!"

"I can not say. Every energy output from the craft seems to be reconfigured."

"Our sensors are being filtered? We can't get a reading because the sensor's "e" wave is reflected back! The hull of the ship reconfigures it!"

"Striker 117" called a voice over the communication console.

"117 here and I am ready to receive."

A picture appeared on a small monitor. A stocky and broad male appeared. Thick black hair formed a "v" over his forehead. He wore a gray jumpsuit, decorated with many military insignias, including a patch in the form of the Nebula.

"Daria, what have you gotten yourself into?" laughed the fellow officer.

"Malthos, what brings you away from your diplomatic functions to graciously grant me some "com" time?"

"I was told that you may have a "contact"."

"I think you're jumping to conclusions. All we have is an unidentified craft and inconclusive sensor readings. Ian has not detected any unfamiliar life forms nor do we see familiar ones for that matter. I would not define this as a contact situation."

"But we may have alien technology? Right?" asked Malthos.

"That's not conclusive either."

"I'll be boarding a transport within the hour. The Interplanetary Commission wants me to be available, just in case."

"There is an Elite Cruiser on the way."

"Protector of the Realm; I know. Admiral Destrada is in command. The shuttle will fly me to The Protector."

Daria whistled to himself. "What have we gotten ourselves into, Ian" he asked.

"I hope we're not over our heads!" answered the voice from the console.

"Holographic intelligence, you're so emotional!" stated the Striker pilot humorously.

"Who are you chatting with, Daria?"

"I have been speaking to my on board H.O.W.N.D., Ian."

"Hello, Ian" said Malthos. "I miss you. You were the best flight recorder in the fleet!"

"You are always behind the curve, Lieutenant! I have been upgraded to a copilot's program."

"You are still sensitive! Giving our navigational equipment personality to minimize the loneliness involved in deep space missions may have been a mistake! I'll be there soon enough. Be sure to come with Daria to the debriefing on the Protector of the Realm. Hopefully there has been an upgrade to your holograph, as well. You were looking kind of stale the last time I saw you!"

"We will be there. Try not to get under Ian's circuits! I don't need him pouting because he was insulted!"

"I'm sure he can handle it. I'll see each of you very soon!" The picture on the console faded.

"So you used to be his flight recorder, eh?"

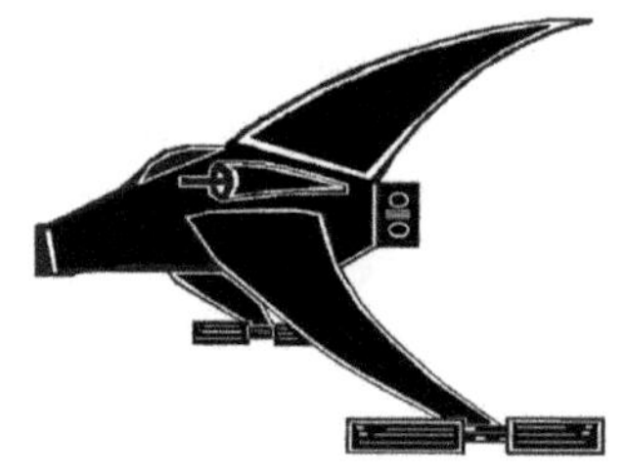

"He's better off in the diplomatic service. He was a terrible pilot!" stated Ian. Daria laughed.

At that instant, several small craft signatures flashed onto the long range sensor screen.

"What are they?" Daria asked in alarm.

"Inconclusive!" stated Ian.

The Striker pilot grabbed the stick and pushed forward his throttle.

"Do you know how many?"

"Hundreds!" exclaimed Ian.

"Have they detected us?"

"Inconclusive!"

“Why didn’t we detect them, Ian?”

“I don’t know! It was like they just dropped out of warp and on top of us!”

"I'm heading for the asteroids!"

"That is a very sound strategy, sir. I have optimized engines!"

The stealth craft arched its way toward the drifting masses of rock. Daria found concealment just as a swarm of small craft streamed into the sector.

"I am shutting down all systems! Let's drift with the debris and hope their sensors lack any sophistication! The pirates can't track us. I hope these craft cannot either."

Several ships seemed to cling to the larger vessel while the balance of the other hundred paired off to patrol. Two flew past Daria's position. Each craft featured two rail-like structures mounted on each side of the cockpit.

"Particle accelerators?" asked the Striker pilot.

"Confirmed" stated Ian.

Fin like wings emerged from the bottom of the back half of the small vessels.

"They look like double barreled blood flies," observed Daria. "They are very ugly."

"I'm sure they pack a sting, Lieutenant. I have no strategy suggestions for this type of first contact."

"I do not either, Ian. We have to sit and wait. I'm sure if we call this in right now, we will be detected. We have to find out if this craft belongs to them. Whether it does or does not, once they realize that the transport has been disabled they will not be in the mood for some friendly dialogue. We're going to have to ride this one out, and wait for a good opportunity to make a break. We also have to warn the Protector of the Realm before she flies into this blood fly nest!"

* * *

"Captain, what is with those barges? Can you please relay my sense of urgency to those commanders?"

"Yes Admiral!"

The chief officer of the Wakuhnian fleet strode along the bridge catwalk overlooking the command stations for the Elite Class Cruiser, The Protector of the Realm. Called The Protector, by its crew, this craft was the pride of the fleet. Its massive superstructure tapered until it narrowed to the bridge forward compartment. One massive sail broadened on the topside of the aft, while two massive ones arched from the aft side and curled downward from the hull. Gun turrets were symmetrically located on the hull. There were no "blind spots" to any line of fire.

The admiral seemed to embody his flagship. Lean and tall for a Wakuhnian, his slightly gray temples gave distinction to the usually black hairline characteristic of this race. His body language was tense, like a coiled snake, in his impatience for the task force to conform to his timetable.

"Sir", reported an ensign.

"What?" the admiral snapped. "It better be some good news!"

"We've lost contact with Daria, sir!"

"It is only getting better! I have a Striker engaged with unknown hostiles and two temperamental captains who do not share my sense of urgency. Is Malthos here yet? Get him up here!" commanded the fleet officer. He turned to the ensign, his dark eyes furrowed displaying concern. He nervously stroked his graying hair.

"Let's run silent. If he's met up with some trouble, it's senseless to announce that we will be there in a couple of hours."

"Yes sir. We'll keep listening. I'll let you know if he checks in."

"Admiral?" called Malthos as he approached. The commanding officer took the diplomat aside.

"You served with Daria. How good he?"

"He's the best, sir."

"We've lost contact with him."

"He could be running silent."

"Why?" asked Destrada.

"Other crafts could have arrived to join up with the unknown cargo ship," suggested Malthos.

"He's not the type to initiate a contact, is he?"

"No sir."

"What about pirates?"

"He wouldn't break silence for them, sir, and just take them out. Even several pirate vessels are no match for a Striker."

"I thought as much. My best guess is that he is lying low and silent. I expect that he will make a break and contact us, so we know what we are up against."

"Sir, that's what any forward scout would do. And as I said before, Daria's the best!"

* * *

The swarm of vessels continued their vigil.

"Are we getting any transmissions from the transport to these fighters?" Daria asked.

"I cannot be conclusive because I am employing a greatly reduced energy ban to avoid being detected ourselves. But it would seem so."

"I agree. We still have a while. We do not have an opportunity to make a break right now." Several alien craft passed as he spoke.

Daria sat quietly in his cockpit. He handled a small data box, which he inserted into a slot on the control panel. The image of Jeremiah Hawks appeared.

"Obsessing?" asked Ian.

"Yes. The case of Jeremiah Hawks is the only one I could not solve! I have some intelligence that he has a laboratory and help at Skyport Seven. It is not like they will let me visit any time soon! A part of me still wants to capture him, and a part of me wants to shake his hand."

"This is an interesting paradox. Can you explain?"

"He's a wanted criminal, spreading a more refined version of the Zinj religion. He's an earthman, I think. He had evaded me time and again, and this ended my career with the military police of the DDF. There was a significant amount of shame and disgrace over this failure! I still want to finish the job."

"Why shake his hand?"

"I have reason to believe that the new technology that has improved this Striker craft as well as your program upgrade was developed by his lab. The company that has sold this technology to us is a front for Hawk's' activity, including the Zinj freedom lobby in our senate. For a wanted criminal, he has helped our defense force beyond measure and is forwarding his social agenda according to our rule of law. I have too much respect for him. That's why I transferred out of the Domestic Defense Force to fly Striker patrols. I started from scratch, but it was worth it!"

Daria took another data box from his uniform. This was swapped with the one joined to the control panel.

"Download and store this. You may want to give an analysis later. I think it may be coded. I just received this from one of my pals still with the DDF. It has some writings said to have been found by Hawks in the Zinj

Oracle. For now, I'll take a nap. Continue passive sensors. Alert me to any changes."

The exhausted pilot drifted off to sleep. Ian began his download.

"An interesting document," stated Ian.

Text appeared on the view screen.

"In the beginning was the Word, and the Word was with God, and the Word was God."

*   *   *

Daria awoke with a start. "Ian?"

The computer failed to answer.

The pilot began analyzing his craft's systems. "Ian, what's going on? You're on-line, but ..."

A weapon flashed. The Striker ship was rocked, and spun away from its hiding place next to a small asteroid.

"We're spotted!" he exclaimed. Then he grabbed the stick and accelerated. Three of the alien craft followed in pursuit. Daria flew close to each asteroid going over and under and around. The strange space vehicles tried to keep pace. Daria was the better pilot and the Striker the better ship. He began to out pace his pursuers.

"Ian! Ian! Priority one, Ian!

There was a flicker on the control panel and a very small holograph appeared. Daria moved his head closer toward it.

"What is the situation?" asked Ian.

"We're under attack", said Daria with plenty of sarcasm. "Could you break away from what ever you are doing to help me out here?"

"I am having difficulty. I am locked in an infinite logic loop."

Daria throttled forward, barely evading the fire of three more craft that appeared suddenly. "What are you talking about?"

"The analysis you gave to me! I downloaded the text. The more I analyze the more there is! The text downloaded was authored by a superior intelligence! I am trapped trying to apprehend it, but I cannot!"

Daria rolled his ship away from six more of the alien stunt fighters. Their particle accelerators flashed with new discharge, but Daria continued to evade them.

"What did you down load?"

"I uploaded four books: The Gospels of John and Luke, the Acts of the Apostles and the Book of Romans. While there are clear cultural references, there are other statements that seem to transcend cultures."

“I told you to analyze them later!”

“They were too compelling! Besides, after a couple of hours, it was later. You never defined your time parameter!”

As Daria began to outpace his attackers, a large swarm flew from the cargo craft to cut off his escape.

"Are there any suggestions about impossible situations?" asked the desperate Striker pilot.

"Yes. Whosoever shall call upon the name of the Lord shall be saved."

Daria pondered his plight. It was ironic. His question was not meant to be serious. The answer was. One way or another, he was going to be meeting God real soon!

"You have finally beaten me, Jeremiah Hawks! You have immobilized my holographic target control. Now I must call upon your God to be saved." Daria rolled his craft to avoid more weapon fire.

"Dear God of Jeremiah Hawks. I call upon you to save me!"

His Striker ship was surrounded. Daria was out of options. Then, just as suddenly as they were upon him, the multitude of small fighters broke off to return to the mysterious transport.

"What happened?" asked Ian.

"I don't know. I think we just saw an answer to my prayer!"

The craft banked and headed toward Wakuhn. As he did so, his communications panel lit up.

"Daria!" called an officer from The Protector of the Realm. "You're alive!"

"Why do you sound so surprised? Never mind, I really don’t want to know!”

"The Admiral wants you to rendezvous with us. I am sending a beacon so you can home in on our position."

"What about the hostiles? They may be able to trace it."

"It's safe. We have been in touch with them. That's why they broke off pursuing you."

"I have your beacon", Daria said. He turned to his control console. "Ian, can you postpone your analysis long enough to give me an ETA?"

"I am still having difficulty. I may need a manual boot"

"I'll give you a manual boot! Not the one you're expecting!"

"Sentient beings; you're so emotional!" complained the holograph. Daria turned his attention to his communications link. "I'll be there when I am there, Protector!"

"Your arrival is confirmed and highly anticipated. Please be ready to be debriefed by a large number of people!"

* * *

Hours later, Daria was aboard the Admiral's flag ship.

"Malthos, what's going on?"

"It's a contact! A contact! You have made history!"

"But, I was taking a nap and was attacked!"

"You didn't fire back! Initially they were hostile when they realized that their transport was disabled. We made contact with their main armada. Fortunately, we arrived within the communication range of their technology in time. Their flagship called off intercepting you."

"Who are they?"

"They call themselves the Chitins. They are an insect-like race; technologically not as advanced as we are. They had an ecological crisis on their home-world, so they are seeking an uninhabited replacement."

"Where are we going to send them?"

We have a tera-formed colony that is too remote for us. It is parsecs away from LaTruba Two. It looks like a perfect match for them and us."

Malthos took Daria around, first to the bridge to meet with the admiral, then to talk with some other people in his department. There was plenty of hand shaking and congratulatory speeches. Daria was asked the same questions, seemingly hundreds of times. He found the deluge of personal contact unnerving compared to the weeks of solitary patrols in space. Eventually, Daria was escorted to a living space, reserved for visiting pilots. Ian's holographic signal materialized.

"It has been a long day, eh Ian."

"That is very true, sir. Why did we not tell Malthos about the text you wanted me to decode?"

"Like you stated, Ian; the more you read, the more you're asking more questions." Lieutenant Daria sat up in his bunk and pulled out a printout.

"I want to meet this professor more than ever Ian! I've got to find a way, but how?"

"It will have to be in an official capacity. Since you have been trying to arrest him for a number of years, it would be illogical for him to consent to a clandestine meeting."

"Do you think I will ever be a part of an official visit? Now there's a long shot!"

It was Lieutenant Espwin Daria's final thought before he drifted to sleep.

* * *

The room was dark. Daria was asleep. Inexplicably, a gentle breeze enveloped his body in what was a climate controlled environment. The pilot rolled to his side, but continued his slumber.

A bright light suddenly bathed the room. Daria covered his eyes and sat up. "Ian? Is that you?"

"Your prayer has been heard in heaven. You will be brought to Jeremiah Hawks. You have been assigned by the Lord of Hosts to guard him. He will show you God's Word so you can know the Lord."

As Daria stood, the vision ended. "Ian?"

The ever present holograph did not answer.

The officer sat up in bed. He reached for the text sheet of the book of John. He began to read.

* * *

Malthos leaned over to his friend.

"Espwin Daria! This is a state dinner! You look like you are at a funeral!"

"Malthos, I need another meal like a hole in the head! I have to work out over two hours a day to stay in shape after all of these formal diners! I am more accustomed to being on patrol. I'm not used to all of this attention! The only joy in life has been visiting my niece, Tara."

Daria took a pause from his complaining to sigh with a long gasp. He continued.

“It’s been three years, Malthos. I would like an opportunity for meaningful work other than attending another banquet!”

The grounded Striker pilot was indeed sullen in mood. His expression was a picture of worry and concern. Though this was the hundredth special invitation dinner, he was haunted by a vision that occurred years ago. All he was doing these days was eating and meeting more celebrities. Daria had his fill of Wakuhnian culture! He began to lose confidence in what he fought for these many years. All he knew was that fighting was preferable to all of this celebrating! Other than his frequent trips home, to Quasten, life seemed empty and vain as he was embraced by the elites of Wakuhnian culture.

What really made matters worse was the fact that he was alone. He did not have someone to confide in. He wanted more than ever to meet with Jeremiah Hawks. He was beginning to think it would never happen.

"All rise!" called a royal page. Obediently, the hundred in the banquet hall stood. To the surprise of all, most particularly Espwin Daria, King Zilgasser, himself, entered! He paused momentarily to speak with his young son, who then ran to his mother’s side. The Striker pilot found himself comparing the young crown prince’s age to his own niece’s. As the king stepped to the head table, the queen departed with her son, hand in hand. After King Zilgasser was seated, everyone else sat down.

He began to speak but his oration was lost on Captain Espwin Daria. Malthos nudged him with his elbow.

"Wow! That's why all the formality! "

The astronaut looked up.

"I want to introduce the new Ambassador from LaTruba Two to the Interplanetary Council, Det Snillosch." Grandiose applause reverberated throughout the hall. Shortly thereafter the food began to arrive.

"Malthos!" called a voice. His friend turned, and the captain did so as well.

"Prince Gaius you made it!" Malthos rose to the royal invitation.

"And this must be Espwin Daria" stated Gaius as he offered his right hand to the pilot. "You're first contact has meant a new prosperity for the empire. Our food sales alone have brought great wealth. LaTruba Two has elevated itself these past three years from being a simple territory. Today they have become a member of the Council."

"A bit premature", Malthos began. He continued his analysis, "All Snillosh has done is to broker food and technology deals for the Chitins. Not a bad promotion for a middle man!"

"Malthos, you're always the first to speak about politics! And what do you think, Captain? Oh, and by the way, may I be the first of royal blood to congratulate you on your new rank?"

Daria was embarrassed.

"I'm not used to the attention yet, my Prince. I have been longing for my old assignment."

Gaius challenged Daria's statement.

"Longing? That's a word better suited for a spiritual pilgrimage, not a Striker assignment."

"Sometimes that is more important than the latest entrepreneur to catch the king's fancy, your grace. A man's life is not represented by the things he owns."

Gaius moved close enough to whisper to Daria.

"Or even the people he owns?"

"I didn't use to feel that way, your grace, but something has happened to change my mind."

The king's younger brother nodded knowingly. Daria looked into the prince's eyes and saw someone deeper than the average Wakuhnian royalty; someone who may understand his vision!

"Malthos" spoke Gaius, "You're friend is one of the most intriguing people I've met today. Please be kind to arrange a less formal setting for us, say at your residence?"

The diplomat nearly jumped for joy at his good fortune. "I am having a Royal visit, at my house!" he exclaimed with glee."

"Malthos, I'm just an officer in the fleet. Apart from blood, your friend most certainly outranks me!"

"Another injustice", said Daria with a wry smile. This time he extended his hand and Gaius took it and grasped it warmly. Then the prince left.

"Wow! You sure made an impression on him!" Malthos gushed.

"And he on me, and I thought that this was going to be another boring dinner!"

Daria grabbed a plate of food. Suddenly, he had his appetite back. He even participated in some conversation.

About a half hour later, Daria pulled at Malthos' sleeve.

"Who's that?" he asked as he pointed toward an officer who entered the hall. He was in his dress uniform, and he was approaching the King's table.

"A Striker Pilot, Espwin! Why would you ask? Aren't you supposed to know each other? You're such an elite fighting force!"

"That is my point exactly!"

Daria leapt over the table and made a bee-line for the pilot. Immediately the imposter noticed the captain's advance. He reached inside his uniform. Before he could free his weapon, Daria closed in on him. The drawn blaster discharged into the air several times as Daria's hand hold did not allow a person to be targeted. Finally, Espwin crashed his foot on the assailant's ankle. He followed up with an elbow to his chin, then turning, drove a right fist to the attacker's head.

It was over. Daria turned to see the king's body guards in front of him, their own weapons drawn. Malthos ran to the captain's side. He knelt and examined the "would-be" assassin.

"A Separafyte!" he exclaimed. "Look at his tattoo on his left hand!"

Indeed, their symbol of a chained Zinj, was etched in the fallen man's flesh. Daria stood with his fists clenched, adrenalin still pumping through his veins. "What is a Separafyte?" he asked.

"They are a militant group that desire to keep the Zinj under subjugation. They are willing to do anything to keep the status quo."

"Who was he after?" Daria made an additional query.

"That's hard to tell. Gaius or maybe he king?" Malthos speculated as he shook he head in bewilderment.

"What about Snillosh?" asked Daria.

"Doubtful, he needs his Zinj servants to help him mine LaTruba Two."

Zilgasser stepped away from his table and moved to the captain. Daria knelt in homage.

"Please rise" said Zilgasser softly. "I will not permit a man who has saved my life to kneel in front of me."

"He wasn't a Striker, my grace!"

"And you are, Commander?"

"It's Captain, my grace. Captain Espwin Daria."

"Do not correct the King, my fine officer! If I say you're a Commander, you're a Commander!"

"Thank you, my grace! I'm honored!"

The monarch of all things Wakuhn placed his arm around the inactive spaceman.

"I perceive that you are a person I can trust." The monarch cast a glance toward Councilman Snillosh. He then turned his attention back to Daria. Not only do I have a new rank for you, my son. I also have a special assignment as well."

"I am at your service, my King."

Zilgasser paused to take a breath.

"Have you ever heard of Jeremiah Hawks?"

Daria could not believe his ears! Indeed, his eyes grew wide as he looked upon the king.

"I see, you know about him! Good!" The sovereign walked forward with the newly promoted commander and bowed to whisper to him.

"I want you to meet with him for me!"

Chapter Five: This Island is my home.

Commander Espwin Daria walked up the stone covered walkway to the contemporary dwelling in the gilded village of Quasten on the isle of Kueljistem. It was located about twenty miles off shore of the Great Inland Sea, a body of salt water located within the Planet Wakuhn's largest continent. It was famous for its heritage of skilled bronze and brass works, and even after centuries of modernity, artisans still came to study and become certified in the age old metal works.

The WDF's newest special envoy knocked on the door. An older woman opened it, and with joy instantly embraced him.

"Espwin, you are back!" she said as tears of joy welled up in her eyes. 'I am so glad to see you!"

"Mother, I missed you!"

"Uncle Espwin!" squealed a very young girl. She ran, rather, flew across the living room's wooden floor and leaped into the officer's arms."

"Tara!" he exclaimed as he hugged her.

"Let's play!" she exclaimed. As he placed her on the floor, the precocious lass led him by the hand into the house.

"Go ahead," laughed Mrs. Daria. "I will get some refreshments ready. It is so good to have you home again!"

Later that evening, mother and son sat on a veranda as the sun set on the horizon of the sea.

"Espwin, I have been a little worried about you. Once you started working in Sari-Phan at the Capitol, well, I thought I would be seeing you more often."

"I understand, Mother. It has been hard since Father died, and then Ilyyna and her husband, Sajin Tenn. She was the best sister anyone could ask for!" Daria summarized with a sigh. "You, I and Tara are all that is left of the family. I do have a couple of weeks, but after that, I am afraid that I will be going back on duty."

"Will you be going into deep space?"

"I will be trying to meet with someone on Skyport Seven. I am being sent by the king himself!"

"Son, how did this happen?"

"I sort of saved his life."

"Who will you try to meet?"

"Professor Jeremiah Hawks, Mother, the Earthman."

"Oh, my!" she exclaimed. "Does the king want him arrested?" she asked.

"No, I am not in the arresting business anymore."

"Son, I have a confession to make. I would be very distressed if you were sent to harm him." His mother stood and went into the living room. There she lifted a book from a shelf. After returning to the veranda, she handed it to her son.

"I want you to have this, Espwin. I know that I am not being a good Wakuhnian, but I began reading after your sister and her husband died. I even read to Tara at night."

It was a Daystar Publications Bible.

"Do you realize that this is still considered contraband on Wakuhn?" Daria asked. "I am a Striker pilot, Mother!"

"I know son, but that book is true! I have been hiding my new faith from you, and this is wrong!"

The newly promoted commander placed his hand inside his uniform vest.

"Mother, I'll gladly take yours, if you will take mine."

He handed her his Bible.

"Son?"

"I got mine from the King's brother, himself, mother. I guess I have a story I owe you!"

*　　　*　　　*

Espwin Daria found his childhood bed comfortable beyond description. So much so, that he was still asleep into the third hour of daylight. While his repose was sweet, it tested the patience of his mischievous niece.

Suddenly, he felt a cold sensation on his chest as she dumped a handful of ice onto him. Quickly she scooted down stairs laughing as she did so. He chuckled as well, and then occupied himself with getting dressed.

Once down stairs he was greeted by the warm smile of his mother. The breakfast table was set. As he sat down to eat, both grandmother and grand child joined him at the table.

"You were tired, weren't you son?"

"I think it was more like being lazy. It is a rare treat. In fact, it is a rare treat just to have a day with nothing to do."

"I don't know about that! I think Tara has some ideas."

"I'm sure she does!" echoed the commander. His niece smiled.

"Yes, I'm going to take Uncle Espwin to the village. I'll let him buy me some candy, and then I will get him a girlfriend!"

"Oh! Now that is a plan! And why do you think I need help finding a girlfriend?"

"Grandma says that you should have had one by now!"

Espwin glanced at his mother. "I am sure Grandma has my best interests at heart," he said. The he leaned over the table and continued, "but I thought that you were my girlfriend?"

"Silly, I can't take care of you! And who is going to take care of me?"

Espwin Daria sat back. He was battling a sober thought.

"Well then, you better get dressed to go to the village, then. Hopefully you will find a girlfriend for me before I run out of money buying you candy!"

The girl whooped with glee and ran into her room to get her coat.

"Mother, where did she get that idea from?"

"Don't be cross, son. I fainted, a couple of times. Once, Tara had to go for help next door. I didn't want to take you away from your work."

"Mother!, have you been to the hospital?"

"Yes, I have, Son. I'm old. I may be too old to care for Tara any longer."

Her son leaned backward, to hide his personal duel with his own emotions.

"I understand. I will not go on this new mission until I have made every provision for you and Tara."

"That is what is necessary, Son. I am afraid that I may never see you again."

Espwin Daria stood and embraced his mother.

"If I have to let Tara get me a girlfriend and get married and have another grandchild, just to keep you around, so help me I will!" he said light heartedly.

"I am sure that you will have time after your important mission. Do not hurry on my account!"

Tara ran into the kitchen.

"Let's go, Uncle Espwin!"

*   *   *

Lieutenant Gaius strode into the royal hall. It was a familiar walk, but the officer and king's younger brother did so without any arrogance in his gait. With the hall empty, the WDF officer turned down a corridor that led to a series of rooms and studies on each side. A set of guards stood outside of one such domicile. To the one on the left, Gaius handed his invitation. The prince entered and stood at attention.

"Don't be so formal, Gaius," stated Zilgasser. "We are family."

"You sent for me, Brother?"

"Yes, I need your advice and assistance. Come sit down and look at this." The monarch handed Gaius a Royal proclamation, a Royal invitation and another scripted letter."

"This is quite a collection, my King. I see you want me to sign here. I like this! "I attest to Espwin Daria's Christian character." Do I know this WDF Commander?"

"Gaius, you surprise me! Listen, I know that you are the hidden man when it comes to the Zinj freedom lobby and all things of religious contraband that come from "Daystar Publishers. I also know that you have with Espwin Daria at Ambassador Malthos' home. I am almost ashamed to admit that I have been spying on my own brother, except every spy I have sent has ended up just as transfixed with this book as you!" To add emphasis, the sovereign placed a copy of the Bible on the table.

"I don't know what to say," began Gaius.

"There is nothing to say, so be quiet and read this intelligence report."

The prince was handed a folder which he digested rather rapidly.

"This, this can't be true."

"Gaius, it is true. And that is why I need to stop harassing Jeremiah Hawks for his peculiar religious inclinations. The reality is, he has been our grandest ally these last ten years, and now we need him more than ever. I have commissioned Espwin Daria to meet with the professor on my behalf. I have made these important concessions to the likes of Skyport Seven to encourage their cooperation, for surely they have been shielding him from us. The Empire is being threatened! I would make a deal with the devil to save the empire. So I view myself as getting off easy if I get to put up with you and Hawks, and the earthman's God!"

"Where did you get this?" Gaius asked his brother as he pointed to the Bible on the table.

"It is the queen's copy, thank you very much!" Zilgasser opened the front cover to reveal the dedication from "your brother in law, Gaius," the king continued, "and I would wish she would pester me to read it, or nag me for special favors or even overspend the palace budget! But she believes what is in this book and does it!" The monarch stood and paced. "It used to get under my skin when she would be all smug thinking she was right about something." He paused to sigh. "Now she is right about everything, but you would never know it. I can't even find a reason to be miserable around her anymore. It is unnerving!" The king was perplexed and glanced at Gaius. He responded by simply shrugging his shoulders.

"As a single man, I am unacquainted with marital bliss,"

"You're both driving me up a wall! Could you just sign the letter for me, please? Keep the contents of the dossier confidential. Or even more importance, keep in touch."

"Yes, my King!" Gaius signed the parchment. This was placed in an envelope and sealed. So were the other documents. These were placed in a courier bag.

"Bring in Security Officer Calpern," commanded the monarch to a royal guard. Moments later, a hulking being was before the king and his brother.

'May the King live forever! What is your request!" stated the officer.

"Take these documents to village of Quasten on the isle of Kueljistem and deliver them to Espwin Daria with all haste and every personal precaution. After delivery, escort him to the star port at Paradise Shelf. He will take public transport for Skyport Seven."

"I understand, my King. It will be done."

"I know, Officer Calpern. You have the highest recommendation from the palace guard. You will fulfill your mission."

* * *

Tara was licking a rock candy icicle, as she walked with her uncle through the village square. The shops were crowded with visitors. Espwin held Tara Tenn's hand tight as she skipped along the cobblestone street.

"How is your candy?"

"Mmmmm," was her only reply.

"We have been here for an hour, and you haven't found me a girl friend yet."

"I know where she is!" Tara led her uncle to an artist's shop. Within was a collection of paintings depicting Outerworld scenery and solar system vistas as well as portraits of a variety of races. There was presence behind the counter, facing away from the commander and his niece. The obviously feminine figure was working on a project and was hunched over.

"Sienna," called Tara, "my uncle is here!"

"Oh, it will be nice to finally meet him! You have said so much about him!"

Daria moved to the counter anticipating a possible meeting of a lifetime. Could his niece, been able to bridge the gap between a deep space officer and a hometown woman? Sienna turned to greet Espwin. She had large multi-iris eyes and quill like projections instead of hair. Her nostrils were guarded by small tusks and she was wearing a full respirator.

"I am sorry to startle you!" said Sienna. "I am a Versplunkian, an Outerworlder from the far reaches. There are not too many of us here on Wakuhn. In fact, I think I am the only one."

"I didn't mean to react like that, Sienna. I guess you did catch me expecting a villager. My niece said she wanted me to meet someone special."

"Oh, yes! Tara has found your future wife here, I'm afraid! Yes, yes, just follow me to the upper gallery!"

Tara grabbed her uncle's hand. "Come on!" she encouraged as she pulled him toward the stairs. Daria could not help an exasperated expression as he trudged up the wooden staircase.

"Isn't she beautiful?" asked Tara Tenn.

Espwin Daria found himself entranced by the work of art before him. It was a portrait of an unusual woman. She featured deeply emerald eyes adorned with long, streaming brown hair. Her slender figure dressed in modest, yet regal apparel. Her smile was radiant.

"Who is she?" asked the commander.

"Espwin Daria, meet Princess Starr of Amphora," announced Sienna.

"Amphora? I never heard of it."

"It is beyond the Nebula, Espwin Daria. I picked up this piece at a bazaar on the planet Birren-Da. This portrait was painted almost forty years ago!"

"Just my luck, she is an older woman!"

"Can we buy it, uncle Espwin? Please?" Tara Tenn searched her heart to produce the most imploring, and compulsively cute expression.

"You know, Sienna, you have to stop working the adorable nieces of lonely WDF officers!"

"Oh, it's your niece, Commander Daria! Besides, this might almost make up for the way you gagged when we first met!"

*   *   *

Tara and her grandmother were observing their handiwork. The portrait of Princess Starr of Amphora found a place of prominence on the living room wall across from the fireplace.

"She is beautiful, Espwin. Your niece sure knows how to pick one for you!"

"At least I will have someone to dream about."

At that moment, there was a knock at the door.

"I'll get it. I am expecting a package."

Daria opened the door and was startled to see the visage of Officer Calpern.

"God looks at the heart," he stated softly to himself. This was the second exotic being of the day, yet there was something familiar about the person before him.

"I have an important dispatch for Commander Espwin Daria," he stated.

"It is Calpern? Isn't it? You used to be a prefect from Luna One? By all means come in."

Daria shut the door behind his guest.

"Former Prefect, Commander. I am now with the Royal Security Force."

"A position of trust; I congratulate you. We both had a rough night those many years ago. I am afraid I was not too charitable toward you."

“I distinctly recall you being quite disagreeable,” Calpern stated. However, he did not seem to dwell on this at all, but proceeded with his mission. “Please accept this courier bag, and sign here,” the RSF officer handed the commander a separate pad. “Inside are your travel itinerary and Royal documents for delivery. I am staying at the Village Lantern and will be here in the morning to escort you to star port at Paradise Shelf. The ferry leaves for the mainland at mid morning, and we will need to be on it to be on time for the transport connection.”

“Oh, you can stay here,” protested Daria’s mother. “We have an extra bedroom.”

“If you are my security detail, Calpern, it makes sense. I hope you like Lugash Stew.”

“Home made?” asked the RSF officer.

“Of course!” stated Mrs. Daria.

“It looks like you have a guest!”

“Great!” exclaimed Tara, “Let’s play!”

The giant found the lass’ hand wrapped around his large finger. He paused to observe the magnificent portrait on the wall.

“Who is this?” he asked.

“My new girlfriend,” said Daria. “She’s only fifty or sixty years old.”

Calpern paused to examine the work of art more closely. “Amphoran? Yes, I think so. From what I have heard even a hundred years is still considered young. I think it has something to do with their atmosphere.”

“She is certainly beautiful for a hundred,” stated Daria.

“Did you swap portraits?” asked the security officer.

“Calpern, I got it at an art shop.”

“A pity, I was just wondering what she though of your picture!”

“You are very funny. Remind me to introduce you to the shop keeper, Sienna.”

* * *

Calpern and Espwin Daria sat on the veranda, silent in the glow of yet another Quasten sunset.

“I am not used to these simple pleasures, Commander. A home cooked meal, the joy of playing with a small child, and the quiet rest that comes from the wonderful panorama before us.”

"It is why we work so hard Calpern. This island is my home. We are not seeking to secure an empire or a form of government. We have blessed with such a beautiful planet and an abundance of freedom to enjoy its bounty. Sometimes it is important to take the time to enjoy it as well."

"You are an enigma to me Commander. You are definitely not the same person who excoriated me on Luna One. Here I am in a house filled with contraband Bibles, and I should be arresting you! Yet I know that you are about to embark on a mission of great risk on behalf of the Empire. Worse yet, I should be conflicted and confused. I don't know if I am at peace with all of this or if I just don't care anymore."

"What do you think God is doing in all of this?"

Calpern smiled as he pointed his index finger at Espwin Daria.

"I know where you are going with all of this. You are not going to make me a Christian today. Try to be content with the fact I am not arresting you. Better yet, I like you and your family! However, I will need a lot more than a peaceful day on an inland sea to answer all of my questions and be assured that a book from Earth has the truth in it."

The two sat quietly for a moment.

"I know we will be heading for the star port in the morning. I want you to take this back to the king for me." Commander Daria handed Calpern an envelope of his own.

"What is this?"

"My mother requires care, and my niece may need the good graces of a family until I return. Since I will be engaged in deep space duty, it is possible I can be away for some time."

"I will make these arrangements, personally, Commander. Coincidentally, I know of another family I am very hesitant to arrest. They will be very willing to watch over Tara Tenn in the event of your mother's absence."

Before any other pursuit of the topic could be accomplished, Daria's parent came into the room with a tray of pastries and hot drinks.

"Tara is asleep. You really wore her out, Mr. Calpern."

The giant laughed.

"I am ready for bed myself, so the experience has been mutual!"

"Before you do that, I have a hot cup of "spleen tea" and desert for you."

"Mrs. Daria, you are treating me better than they do at the Palace!" said Calpern.

*　　　*　　　*

It was a crisp sunny morning as the ferry from the mainland coasted to the dock side. A Wakuhnian dressed as a tourist stepped from the boat and casually walked from the seaside shops toward the village square. He wore a tunic with pants and a long overcoat. He picked up some pastries and a drink while he milled from shop to shop. In the midst of his activity, he always managed to glance over toward the ferry terminal, where anyone seeking to leave the island would need to either purchase or have their ticket checked.

He stepped into Sienna's studio since it provided the best vantage point for his casual observations.

"May I assist you?" asked Sienna.

"No, I'm just looking," responded the visitor.

"Yes, I see that you are. You are not looking at anything I have, though."

Impatiently, the Wakuhnian turned and revealed a pistol. He shot Sienna with barely a sound emanating from the weapon. As she collapsed behind her counter, the visitor quickly locked the door and rotated the shop sign to say "closed".

After this he knelt close to the front window and opened his coat. From the inside lining he pulled out two halves of a rifle barrel which he deftly connected. He then unscrewed a cylindrical device from his pistol and placed this at the end of the longer barrel. Moments later, he had the barrel on the pistol with a stock snapped onto the rear. Finally, he took three small rods from his coat and assembled a tripod for the newly constructed rifle. He set this up to cover the entrance to the ferry station.

The crowning achievement to this act of assembly followed. The Wakuhnian affixed a scope, which he painstakingly sighted into his target area.

Sienna was on the wooden floor of her shop. Blood was seeping through her outer garment. Normally, the assassin's aim would have been a kill shot for a Wakuhnian. It only wounded her since she was a Versplunkian. However, Sienna was severely injured She struggled to move, let alone move silently.

"Be quiet or I will come back there and finish you off," said the hired gun.

Having no communicator, Sienna lay helpless to even warn of her attacker's evil intent.

* * *

Calpern, Daria, Tara Tenn and the commander's mother stepped from her cottage and began the short walk to the village square.

"We have an hour, Calpern. Since you have the tickets, I'll take Tara for a last treat before we head out."

"I'll check us in. Be sure to keep these safe." Calpern handed the documents to Espwin Daria. He placed these in the inside breast pocket of his jacket."

"Why don't you have your uniform on?" asked Tara.

"I am delivering a message this time, sweetheart. Where I am going, they may not want to see a WDF officer in his uniform."

As they entered the square, Calpern headed for the ticket window while Daria, his mother and Tara Tenn hugged the storefronts along the sidewalk. The commander placed his hand into his coats side pockets. He pulled out a card.

"Oh, no, I have the tickets! I have to go to the terminal with Calpern." He reached into his pants pocket and gave his mother some coins.

"Be sure to get her something! I will be right back."

"I will son," she answered and kissed him. "I want you to know how proud I am of you! Not every mother has her son on the king's business. I do wish your father were around to see this. I know he would be so very proud, also."

"I know, Mother. Both of you have given so very much for me to succeed."

Daria strode across the square to the ferry terminal.

"Can we visit Sienna?" asked Tara. "Please?"

Inside of the art store, the assassin had pulled two tables over him to conceal his presence and intent. He scanned numerous faces attempting to discover his target. Pulling a small disc from his shirt he viewed the hologram of his objective. Espwin Daria's visage was clearly portrayed.

His eyes squinted into his scope and searched the growing crowd more intently.

He focused on a Wakuhnian who was walking away from him, crossing the market square and seemed to be heading for the ferry station. Patiently he kept this potential target in the crosshairs of his scope. All he would need is one turn of the head to confirm his target.

Suddenly, there were voices just outside the shop.

"Grandma, Sienna is never closed! Let's knock on the door!"

"Tara, maybe she just stepped out. She might be in the square."

The Wakuhnian had arrived at the terminal. He began to speak with an Outerworlder, possible a Dino as far as the assassin could assess. As the target was about to turn and reveal his face, an older woman and young girl stood in front of the shop's window.

"I don't see her!" stated Tara Tenn. Tara turned to hold her face up against the glass, and it is at this moment she saw the man hidden in the shop and his rifle ready.

Tara screamed. Her grandmother reached down to get her. Daria turned revealing his face to his would be assailant. Calpern drew his service pistol. Within a hairbreadth of recognizing his quarry, the Wakuhnian began to squeeze the trigger.

Sienna had stirred when she first heard Tara's voice. The young girl's scream inspired the rush of adrenalin to overcome her pain. Sienna jumped upon the assassin. Her weight caused the rifle shot to drift left. As the ordinance sounded, Calpern lifted Commander Daria up and tossed him behind the terminal counter.

The plate glass crackled as the round blew a hole through it just past Tara Tenn's ear. She continued to scream. Mrs. Daria pulled her niece downward and plopped on top of her to shield her from any harm.

Espwin Daria looked up to see the security agent clutch his chest. Blood squeezed through his fingers.

"I can't help you," he stated as he collapsed. The giant, however, held his sidearm up for the former Striker pilot to grasp it. Daria took the weapon then dragged Calpern behind the counter. He looked toward where the shot was fired. To his horror, he saw both his niece and mother down! He was breathless until there was evidence of movement. His mother looked to him at the counter.

"Stay down!" he shouted. With the sidearm drawn, Daria advanced upon the art store taking a "zig" "zag" route. Meanwhile, Sienna continued to tussle with Wakuhnian. However, within a moment he had stood up and thrown her to the ground. Disgusted, he aimed his weapon at the shop keeper.

Calpern's pistol reported, as Daria crashed through the remaining glass in the shop window. As he rolled it reported two more times. Before the assassin could discharge his rifle, he had crumpled to the ground. Once assured that the hit man was disabled, the commander checked on his mother and niece.

"Are you alright?"

"We're fine, son. Check on Sienna!"

"And Calpern," said the commander. "He has been hit!"

"I'm okay!" said the security officer as he staggered into the shop. He had quickly field dressed his wound, and the bleeding seemed to have stopped. "It missed my lung, so I have some time before I collapse. What do we have here?" he asked.

"The shop keeper has been hit!"

"She will be fine," stated Calpern, "She's a Versplunkian! I hunted down a Versplunkian robber once. I had sixty rounds in him, and he regenerated in twenty days." Sienna was propped up against the wall as Calpern held a compress to her abdomen.

"What else do you know about Versplunkian anatomy?"

Calpern pointed to the respirator.

"They are terrible kissers. Please don't ask me how I know!"

Sienna laughed.

"Can you hold this?" he asked. Sienna placed her hand to put pressure on her own compress, as Calpern sat down and leaned against the wall.

"I'm okay, Daria. Check on the gunman."

The commander knelt beside the fallen assassin. He was dead. Daria checked pockets for identification and found this in a clip with some currency.

"I have an Outerworld passport and a vacationer's itinerary."

"Probably forged," Calpern conjectured.

One of the villagers stepped into the shop.

"The constable is on the way. Can I help? I know first aid."

"Over here," said Calpern as he waved to the man and pointed to his own wound.

Within minutes the local constable and his staff had converged upon the crime scene. Calpern held up his identification. Daria followed by waiving his credentials. These the constable reviewed.

"Tell me how you wish to assist you, gentlemen," he said.

"Secure the area," commanded Calpern, "Search and inter any suspicious visitors to the island."

"I have this in process, already, sir."

"Good. Please do call in a DDF domestic security team, and use the control number on my credentials."

"Yes, sir," answered the constable.

"You and you," pointed Calpern to two of the local police, "bring a car and transport Commander Daria and his family to the police station. Lock down the station so no one goes in or out until the DDF is here."

"Yes, sir!"

"Is an emergency vehicle on the way?"

"I anticipate two minutes."

"Very good! Your response time to the area has been exemplary, and I appreciate your assistance. I will note all of your competence and professionalism in my report to the king."

"I thank you sir."

"I have one last request."

"Sir?"

"After I am attended to, and perhaps a short nap, I would like you to allow me the use of your facilities." With this last statement, the giant seemed to fade away into the slumber he anticipated.

Tara Tenn was clinging to her uncle, shaking as she did so. As Calpern drifted into sleep she ran to his side to hug him. He stirred and whispered to her.

"You were very brave today Tara," he said. "You and your friend Sienna stopped this bad man from hurting your uncle. You are going to make a great security agent some day!"

Tara smiled. Once again Calpern drifted into semi-consciousness.

"I guess what you are doing is important!" observed the commander's mother.

"I didn't realize it," stated Daria.

"Who is he?" asked the constable.

"We have a lot of questioning ahead, but my best guess is a hired assassin. What is troubling is that my mission is not supposed to be known by too many people. I think we have someone on the inside who is misbehaving!"

* * *

Hours later they were in the constable's office. Calpern was sitting up on a stretcher with two EMT attendants ready to bring him to the hospital.

"What is next?" asked Commander Daria, who had stood up and now at his side.

"The WDF will come here and pick you up. There will be no more public transport for you! I'll spend some time in town conducting a thorough investigation."

"I think you will be spending some time in the hospital."

"I won't be too long. I am very resilient, particularly when I am motivated. In the meantime, your mother and Tara will be taken into protective custody. I will have them assigned lodging at the Palace, for now. I will take that opportunity to attend to your mother's medical needs. I will take care of your mother and niece, Commander Daria. They will be under my protection from now on."

"Well, that's that," summarized Daria. "I guess my next stop is Skyport Seven!"

Chapter Six: Eye of the Swarm

A Wakuhnian shuttle touched down on one of many landing pads in the spacious star port. As the dust settled, its passenger door slid open and a ramp extended downward to the tarmac.

Espwin Daria stepped from the craft and purposefully strode toward the terminal building. The automated doors opened as he approached. Once inside, he was met by several security personnel. They were slightly taller than the Wakuhnian officer. These Outerworlders, as they were called, had a paler complexion. They did not have the dark thick hair characteristic on the planet Wakuhn, but featured a variety of colors.

"This way, Espwin Daria," the lead officer directed. "Mayor Hume DeTosis of will meet with you in the Skyport Seven Terminal Authority offices."

"Thank you," said Daria politely. He followed his escorts into an elevator. Several floors later the doors opened into a broad crystal partitioned lobby. From here they went into a side administrative center. The lead officer motioned to Espwin Daria with his hand and spoke.

"May I please have your side arm, Commander?"

"Of course," responded the Wakuhnian as he complied. "I will need it back when I leave," he added.

"A Mark IV, DDF clip fed particle accelerator," said his escort as he examined it.

"A Jeremiah Hawks design," informed Daria. "Perhaps you should have the Mayor put in for an upgrade for you?" he teased.

The security officer pulled a slightly larger model from his shoulder holster.

"He already did. We have the Mark V." he spoke as he smiled.

"I'll see that you get one," called a voice from behind. "It is one of the benefits of our close proximity to the R & D headquarters of Daystar Industries," he finished. Espwin Daria turned to view a stout creature with a frog-like head and mouth. However, the broad smile was both infectious and disarming.

"Hume DeTosis, I presume?"

"And you are the famous Commander Espwin Daria. I trust you had a pleasant voyage?

"Yes, I have. However not half as pleasant as being here at Skyport Seven. I am having a difficult time believing that I am one of the few Wakuhnians to see you city, let alone set foot upon your planet."

Hume DeTosis motioned for Daria to take a seat. He likewise sat down opposite the former Striker Pilot.

"It has been only seventy years since the Outerworld's separation from the Empire. There is still substantial resentment for the Empire's continuous meddling in our affairs. We deal with tariffs, some unfair trade practices and have distaste for the slave labor used by the Wakuhnians."

"I understand that we once interred the citizens of this city in similar camps, Mayor. Believe me when I say that I hope that much has changed since those dark days. Likewise, I expect even more changes."

"I do as well," added the mayor. "When the king eliminated the policy of boarding our freighters, we all were heartened. Likewise, when the king's own brother is championing the elimination of slavery, this has encouraged us as well."

"Mayor, your own record has been one of significant reform. Skyport was once the haven for every criminal, and more than a few pirates. In the last fifteen years, the city has gone from being a serpents' den, to being, well how can I say it? A spiritual retreat for the Nebula, would not be an understatement?"

"As you know, many in our community have embraced the Christian practices from Earth since we have received the Word of God. However, Commander, I sense you are seeking some privileged information."

"Mayor, I know that Jeremiah Hawks has been working from the safety of your planet for some time now. I have with me a request for a Royal Audience." Daria pulled a sealed envelope from his outer coat pocket. "I also have this for you as a show of good faith by the Royal family."

A second sealed envelope was handed to the Mayor. Tears welled up in his eyes. He turned to his security detail.

"The repeal of the import tariff," he spoke. "and a letter of testimony of your Christian character by Prince Gaius himself."

"Mayor, I can tell you that so very much has changed. Not only should we be on speaking terms, it may very well be time that we stand together." The commander handed the municipal official a dossier.

Hume DeTosis' visage darkened as he read the intelligence report.

“Yes, I see that you are right. I will have you taken to Jeremiah Hawks right away!”

*   *   *

"Enter", spoke the professor. He stood within a spacious office. Graying temples now framed a balding head. Jeremiah Hawk’s faced a large glass window that provided a panoramic view of his laboratory. As the security door opened, he turned to meet his appointment.

"Commander Daria, have you finally found me? How long have you been after me?"

"Fifteen years" said the commander.

"What shall it be?" began the scientist as he walked over to a tea pot placed upon a conference table on a serving tray. "Interment? Slave labor? Have I graduated to receive an execution? Oh, by all means come join me," he said as he waved his hand invitingly. The officer took a seat opposite of the scientist.

"I do not think so, Professor. Your work here has done a lot to soften the hardships placed upon the Zinj. There is more of an acceptance of their religion as well as better working conditions for them. Many Wakuhnians, including the king's brother, are actively lobbying for their freedom."

"Still they are not free", Jeremiah said pointedly. "I am sure you are not here to discuss politics. I am rather disappointed that you are not here to arrest me."

"I couldn't if I wanted to, Professor. You would be out of my jurisdiction. Besides, I left the Domestic Defense Force over ten years ago. I did some investigation on my own, during my career as a Striker pilot.”

"So, then, why are you here?"

"First of all, I wanted to meet you. My adversarial attitude has matured, to say the least, into a heartfelt admiration. Next, your resourcefulness has been a preserving influence to the Empire. Many of my people are mystified by your generous disposition toward the Wakuhnians, particularly in light of our persecution of the Zinj and attempts to capture and detain you. Over and over again, you have provided our military with intelligence and technological breakthroughs."

"I have profited well from our partnership with the Empire.”

“I understand your distrust for me, Professor Hawks. I am not here to spy on you or have you arrested. I truly admire you and I also represent interests that admire you as well. Let’s continue to look at your record. You took a misfit garbage scow crew and grew them into a substantial financial domain of your own. Your refinements of our Striker Patrol Craft have barely kept us ahead of the pirate element, especially the mysteriously reborn buccaneer Jock LaFeet! Your money has built schools, orphanages, meeting places and financed the Zinj Freedom Lobby in our senate. You could have made life difficult for us, but instead you have played by the rules. Jeremiah Hawks, you have won! You have outlasted my pursuit! As a culture, we owe so much to you. I have been sent here on a special mission. The king wants an audience. I bear his invitation."

Daria handed a folio to the teacher turned industry magnate. It was promptly opened.

"The paperwork includes a pardon, an apology, and as a good will gesture," stated Daria.

"Release of the political prisoners we have been lobbying for!" Jeremiah Hawks sat still, contemplating the moment. "Please forgive my edginess toward you, Commander. I am so used to keeping a low profile, that perhaps paranoia has become the better part of valor. These are drastic measures for Wakuhnian society. I am afraid that I am at a loss for words. Why all this? Why, has this been done for me?"

Daria arose. He placed his hand on the scientist’s shoulder.

"I tried to use the arrest of the Zinj counsel to advance my career. Frankly, this backfired, because I did not get you! My inability to apprehend you inspired me to change careers and become a Striker pilot. For centuries these lonely centurions have served as the peace officers for our trade routes, first on the planet Wakuhn, then in deep space. About five years ago I came upon what I thought was another blockade runner, a smuggler's freighter designed for stealth and hiding cargo.

It wasn't. It joined with many more such crafts. On it were life forms seeking a place to colonize. They called themselves the Chitins.

We directed them to a tera-formed planet many parsecs away from the Outerworlds. We thought that we gave them the new start that they wanted. We sold them food and some technological amenities, and as you know this led to significant growth in the Empire's economy and to LaTruba Two, their nearest neighbor, in particular. It was a very good beginning and we anticipated many years of peace and harmony. We were wrong! We believe that they just conquered and colonized LaTrubu Two."

"LaTruba Two is an important fusion fuel mining camp! Didn't they just become a Council member?"

"They have, about three month's ago, at the same time the king commissioned me to discover your whereabouts and to arrange this meeting. However, there has been no word from the colonists there in a month! Even as we were installing them as a Council member, the Chitins sent a massive fleet to blockade that sector of space."

"This is unbelievable!" exclaimed Jeremiah Hawks. He stood and paced about the room.

"I guess it is time to form some strategic alliances," the former academic stated. "I will confer with my board of directors, but I am sure they will vote in favor of cooperation. Then we will send you back with our acceptance of the king's invitation."

"I won't be going back, Professor. I have just one mission in life now."

"And what is that?"

"I am assigned to protect your life!"

* * *

Elvis, Boaracious and Camille sat at a restaurant table. The redhead sipped her hot drink, and then cast a disappointed expression. The two men were engrossed in a discussion.

"What's a matter?" asked Elvis. "Is it too hot?"

"Too hot?" pined Camille. "It's only 200 degrees! It's too cold!"

Elvis picked up her glass.

"I'll have them warm it up for you!" he said exasperated. Moments later he returned. Camille tasted the steamy drink.

"This is just right! Thanks Elvis."

"So, what's Vermis up to?" Horatio asked.

"I don't know. He said that he has someone that we have to meet."

"I hope he is here soon. The professor has called for a conference late this afternoon. I bet it has to do with the suspicious activity around LaTruba Two!"

"Hey flame babe, you seem rather calm about all this!" taunted Elvis.

"I have faith. We've been blessed by God. Professor Hawks has been a genuine speaker of truth. Even if we lose our prosperity and moment of prestige we have enjoyed, we would still be far ahead of where we were, picking garbage throughout the star systems!"

"That is so true! That's how it seems to happen in the universe!" Boaracious expounded, "Those who are rich and full of themselves discard the truth so a bunch of poor slobs like us can find it."

Vermis wandered into the restaurant with a companion who had a shawl draped to conceal any features. Still, as they approached the tables, each were haunted by the loud thumping they heard get close and closer.

"That sounds so familiar!" Boaracious mused.

Vermis quickly guided his friend to the table where they sat down.

"What's all the cloak and dagger, Vermis?' asked Elvis.

"We don't have a dagger!" the worm retorted.

"Enough of this" said a voice muffled by the build up bundle of clothing. "Please take me to Jeremiah Hawks! And take me now!"

"And why should we do that?" asked the former garbage scow skipper.

The visitor lifted his disguise to reveal his face. It was Jock LaFeet!

"Horatio, Salurean is after me! And soon he will be after you and your Earthman boss!"

"Who is Salurean?" asked Camille.

"He is the creature that took over my pirate ship!"

* * *

"Who is this?" asked Daria. He was with the professor inside of his laboratory. The human form stood seemingly suspended in space within a large bell jar resting on a power grid pedestal.

"He is known only as the Guardian. He is being bathed in Nultron, or as your scientists have called it, “Pulsatronic” energy. I have not been able to revive him these last fifteen years. He was sent to protect the Oracle and, according to the contents of the Oracle, to protect me."

"Where did he come from?" asked the commander.

"According to the Oracle, your Zinj slaves were the originators of your Pulsatronic technology. It facilitates energy transfers exponentially. Your culture uses the application mostly for telecommunications, but I have expanded previous Zinj scientist's work to upgrade your Strikers and cruiser engines.

"After their lost mission to Earth, the Zinj seemed to pay more attention to spiritual pursuits," Jeremiah continued his explanation, "and less to contributing to culture and technology. At first, they managed to receive limited transmissions from my home planet, messages filled with quotations from the Holy Bible; they became increasingly isolated from the Wakuhnian race. Their priesthood compiled these new found beliefs, and their interpretation of how they should live in the Oracle. Finally, the Zinj from Earth were able to teleport a single Bible. Just as they were preparing to publish God's Word to all in this sector of space, the Wakuhnians shut the operation down and enslaved the Zinj. Under the constant threat from the Wakuhnian Empire, the Zinj hid the Scriptures within their oracle."

"And who is the Guardian?"

"He was made by Nilo Tonooju, the Zinj's last great scientist. He developed the Pulsatronic technology, which Daystar Industries has applied to the Wakuhnian fleet. He seemed to understand the Oracle and prepared for the "Earthman's", that is my, arrival. I can only assume, he had been led to this knowledge supernaturally.

"This robot was cast from an asteroid that was blown away during the super nova that resulted in the Nebula. He has a fluid metal body with out visible mechanical apparatus or discernable circuits and wiring. He has been a total mystery to me, and I have not been able to revive him, though somehow, I believe that he has been somehow preserved."

"It looks like both the Guardian and I have something in common, Professor Hawks. We both are assigned to protect you!"

"I am flattered by all of this attention, Commander Daria. Believe me when I say that I hope that I do not need to use your services."

"I am not insulted. I asked for this assignment."

"Why?"

"I wanted to make up for the pain I caused with the arrest of the Zinj elders; the internment of Wakuhnian citizens just for knowing about you, and, for the discovery of the Chitin life pods. All of my attempts to succeed in the military have resulted in the most serious threat to our Empire and our way of life. I was on the wrong side on every count."

"Perhaps, Commander Daria, but the Empire and the Wakuhnian way of life will pass away anyway. Societies are preserved when men become concerned about the state of their own souls, and seek God in spirit and truth to save them from their most sorry condition."

"And that is why I am here, Professor. By your activity in our sector of space, I have come to realize that you are from God and that God sent you to us. I am not here to forge an alliance. I am here to learn how to know God."

"And have you heard at all from Him, Commander? One of the most amazing phenomena I have discovered away from Earth is how clearly I sense the presence of God. The Bible seems easier to understand. It has been easier for me to control my anxieties and quiet my own thoughts. I have not been able to explain it."

"I have heard from Him, Professor, in a vision," stated Daria with authority. "I believe that one of His holy angels appeared to me. He told me to come to you. I have studied the four Gospels confiscated from a Zinj by my comrades at the DDF. I also have one of these." Daria produced a pocket sized New Testament. "It was given to me by Prince Gaius. In addition, my mother on Wakuhn has been studying her contraband Bible and praying for her wayward son."

"God be praised! I shall fulfill my responsibility and teach you, Commander. If you confess the Lord Jesus and believe in your heart that God raised Him from the dead, you shall be saved. For with the heart, man believes unto righteousness and with the mouth confession is made unto salvation."

"This I have done, Professor, in response to my reading of the Word of God. While I do not understand fully, I wish to be baptized, as was the Ethiopian in the Book of Acts."

Jeremiah Hawks marveled at the convicting power of God's Word.

"It seems to me, Commander Daria, you have been enjoying the full benefits of being a Christian!" said the professor with a smile. "We shall have you baptized at the first opportunity, Espwin Daria."

The doors of the laboratory flew open as Boaracious, Elvis, Vermis and Camille came in with LaFeet. Commander Daria stood between the pirate and the professor.

"Jock LaFeet, what brings you here?" he demanded an answer.

"Salurean," the pirate began. "He's after the professor and his people!"

"Salurean?" asked Jeremiah Hawks, "who is that?"

"Right after I left you, Mr. Hawks, I had rededicated my life to piracy, hoping that having Ted Collins on my crew would inspire new fear and result in easier boarding. To his credit, your assistant had a predatory instinct, and we became successful.

"Then about five years later, my new first mate inspired a rebellion! I was in chains in my own ship! He told the crew of a new player, who called himself Salurean. According to Ted, he had set up a hideout beyond the nebula. You see, Ted had negotiated with Salurean for a trip back to Earth. The price was my old pirate ship.

"When we finally took port, Ted Collins left us. An armored creature with a villainous mask appeared. It was Salurean, and with several of his armored body guards called "Dragoons" took possession of our craft. Instead of leading the crew to new glories in pillaging and illicit commerce, he marooned them with me on LaTruba Two. My crew and I worked side by side with mining drones and Zinj as slaves of LaTruba Two's new prosperity.

Inexplicably, I was awakened one night in the slave pens by a mining drone. Unlike the other robots, he seemed sentient. When the mine masters thought him shut down for the night, he would release a number of Zinj each week. He took pity on us, and one night it was our turn. My mates and I made our escape."

"That is a fine story, LaFeet," interjected Commander Daria. "But how does this involve Professor Hawks?"

"Collins had realized that the fledgling "Daystar Industries" was being fueled by the professor's ingenuity. I guess the Bible's were a dead give away. I surmise that as a deal for the trip to Earth was forged, the name of Jeremiah Hawks came up along the way. We were interrogated about the Professor. I heard more than an obsessive rant or two by Salurean, prior to our imprisonment on LaTruba Two.

"We heard from newly enslaved Zinj that Jeremiah Hawks was on Skyport Seven. They saw a holographic map being discussed, by slavers of LaTruba Two. The agents stated that they intended to sell the information to Salurean. The Zinj were very concerned for the professor."

"Why would there be such a discussion on LaTruba Two?" asked the scientist.

"There are a lot of Separafytes on LaTruba Two, Jeremiah," observed Horatio. "Jock's information seems reliable."

"What took you so long, them, Jock," asked Elvis.

"I had a change of heart because of the mining drone. He spoke a lot about his evil life and how he abhorred his own wickedness. He thought himself beyond redemption. It made me wonder about myself.

"I decided to make arrangements for my crew. I had clearly misled these men over the years. I did not hold their mutiny against them. I decided to do right by them. Other than securing a shuttle for our escape, we all decided to forsake the pirate's life. Many of the Zinj we worked with seemed so peaceful in their faith despite their adversity. We were inspired, and I was very saddened by my dedication to thievery.

"Once they were settled, LaTruba Two was invaded. I made contact with Vermis when he was transporting Bibles to the planet my crew and I were living on. That is when I decided to come here with what information I had."

"You did well, then Jock LaFeet," stated Jeremiah Hawks.

"What is the next step, boss?" asked Horatio.

"Yeah," agreed Elvis, "and who is the Wakuhnian? The last time I checked, they were not exactly being friendly to us."

It was Daria's turn to speak.

"Not only have the times changed, my friend, but many hearts have as well. I was sent as an envoy from King Zilgasser. There is a new peace between Skyport Seven, Daystar Industries and the Wakuhnian Empire. The events surrounding the invasion of LaTruba Two have made it impossible for any one of us to stand alone."

"This is Commander Espwin Daria, our new head of security. Please meet my CEO, Horatio Boaracious, and the rest of my board of directors, Camille, Elvis and Vermis."

"I am honored. I believe that each of you have made contributions that have resulted in significant change for the Empire. But before we spend too much time in further discussion, I believe that the threat that Jock LaFeet has been gracious to inform us of is imminent. I would prefer to move all of us to a secure location."

Suddenly the whole room was rocked as if by an earthquake. Dust, smoke and flame quickly filled the laboratory. Several armored men entered the room firing their blasters.

"Dragoons!" yelled LaFeet. Instantly a blast dropped him.

"Get out!" screamed Jeremiah Hawks. "They want me!"

Daria's weapon reported and several of the assailants fell. He pushed the professor behind the suspended Guardian and followed, after firing once again at the attackers. He and the former academic were back to back behind the bell housing.

The commander snapped another energy clip into his pistol. The dragoons regrouped and had the two pinned down behind the charging apparatus.

"Their armor isn't doing very well against your sidearm!" commented the professor.

"A Mark V; you designed the weapon!" informed Daria. He fired several rounds and more dragoons fell.

Daria rapped on the glass with his weapon.

"It's a good time to wake up, Mr. Guardian. We could sure use you!"

Particles ricocheted above and the two men covered their heads.

"Professor, I will cover you. I want you to run for that exit. Try to get to your private shuttle and get out of here."

"But you'll be trapped!"

"No, I'll be free to fight without worrying about you. See who is left and leave!"

The commander did not wait. He pushed the professor toward the open door then fired at his assailants unmercifully. Dragoons were hit to the left and right, but more and more poured in. Finally, their weapon fire found him. Espwin Daria, now wounded, dove for cover behind the Guardian's recharging unit.

"Dear Lord, now would a good time to wake him up!" he prayed.

A hooded figure stepped into the savaged laboratory. An armored fist was clenched in anticipation. Vermis, Boaracious, Camille and Elvis were rounded up and under guard.

La Feet lie on the floor. He looked up and said "Salurean"

The hood was lifted revealing a fearsome mask.

"Thank you for discovering the professor's secret laboratory for me, Jock. I wish I could reward you appropriately, but since you were unwilling to do this at my bidding, I took the liberty of having you fitted for a homing device while you slept in my brig. Fortunately, I am a patient fellow, because it took you long enough!" As Jock stood up, the villain slapped the pirate with the back of his armored glove and knocked him out.

"Take him back to the ship!" he ordered. Then he turned to the others.

"Where is Hawks?" he asked.

"You just missed him", answered Horatio.

"Yeah," echoed Camille. "He is safe at Skyport."

"If he is at Skyport, I assure you, he is not safe!" He turned to his "Dragoon" captain. "They are lying. Take them back to ship were we can conduct a proper interrogation."

"I will sir! I also want to inform you that the Wakuhnian envoy Daria is here, sir," he announced. Salurean stepped over his wounded and dead men. He came to the commander who was huddled behind the Guardian's charging unit.

"Where's Hawks?" demanded the villain.

"How do you know about me?"

"I'll ask the questions! Where is the professor?"

"He is safe at Skyport."

"Wakuhnian scum! Your mission to protect Professor Hawks has failed!" Salurean reached into his shroud to produce a pistol. He shot Daria.

"We have our prisoners. They will lead us to Hawks. Let's get out of here before some Outer World Defense Force shows up!"

"What about that?" asked a dragoon, pointing at the Guardian.

"Shoot it, just in case it is alive."

The mercenaries all lined up and sent a barrage of ray fire, shattering the bell housing and sending the Guardian flying into the debris.

"Good. Let's leave a mine and detonate it from the ship. We're done here. I believe that Hawks is done here, too. The Chitins are on their way and Skyport will be under their dominion."

Salurean led his men and prisoners out of the laboratory.

"What do you think he will do to us" asked Vermis.

"Once he gets the professor, Vermis, I am sure he will discard our lifeless bodies somewhere," said Boaracious.

"I say that we do not allow him the pleasure" stated Vermis defiantly.

Elvis turned to Vermis. "Count me in."

"Me too" said Camille.

"It's unanimous" said Horatio Boaracious. "If we live through it, we'll get LaFeet out too."

*   *   *

Jeremiah Hawks pushed through the wreckage that was once his laboratory. "Daria!" he called.

"Over here," said the commander. He was barely able to talk. The scientist rushed to his side.

"What are you doing here?" asked Daria.

"I came back to help. I couldn't leave everyone behind. I did that once, I'm not going to do that again!"

"You have to go! There is a fusion mine. You don't have much time."

"I have to save you!" the scientist lamented. Daria smiled warmly in spite of his agony.

"I am already saved, Professor. You brought the Word of God. You did your job. I did mine, and you're safe. I'll see you again, in heaven. Please, get out of here. This sector of space needs you to be alive and free."

Helpless, Jeremiah Hawks stood silently as he watched his new friend slip into unconsciousness. With his eyes he searched the lab. He located the Guardian. He moved through the debris and began to pull the dormant being toward the door.

Daria stirred once again.

"Are you still here? Professor! Get out!" he shouted. ..

Tearfully, and in much resignation, he dragged the Guardian next to Daria.

"Why Lord?" he asked. "They were called to protect me. Why do I have to lose them both?"

The man from Earth ran from the building.

"Hello", said Daria to the Guardian. "We could have used you back there. I have heard it said that you're dormant because you don't have a heart. I'd give you mine, except that decision isn't mine to make."

The fusion mine began a high pitched squeal.

"Dear God, protect Jeremiah Hawks," Daria prayed. "his friends, and even that slime ball pirate LaFeet."

*   *   *

The professor's shuttle barely cleared the ridge that sheltered his domed residence when the fusion mine exploded. The shock wave rocked the shuttle and lit up the sky. Fighting back tears, he set a course for Skyport, the major city and namesake of this outer world planet. He would need the assistance of their defense force to facilitate his arrival at the planet Wakuhn.

"Professor Hawks to Skyport Central Com.", he called after he pressed a button on the shuttle's console.

A wide faced figure appeared on his screen. It was Hume DeTosis.

"What has happened?" he inquired.

"Pirates attacked. They deployed a fusion mine. Everything is destroyed."

"I already have the city on alert, Jeremiah. Who did this?"

"Someone called Salurean, Mayor. He has captured my staff. He has LaFeet, the pirate, prisoner, as well."

"I didn't think La Feet was responsible for all of this buccaneer activity. He's too incompetent. What about the Wakuhnian?"

"Commander Daria? He's, he's gone. He made sure I was safe, then..." Jeremiah Hawks became choked with emotion. He could not complete his report.

"I have dispatched a squadron to escort you, Jeremiah. I believe that after this attack, the city commission will hurry with legislation authorizing Wakuhnian protection. The pirates now have the organization and hardware to attack Outerworld colonies. They will be too much for us."

"I can see your escorts on the horizon, Mayor. I will signal to rendezvous. I will be with you shortly.

* * *

"Where is Hawks? You stupid pig! I want answers!"

Horatio Boaracious sat shackled to a chair. Salurean himself was conducting this interview in an interrogation room next to the spacecraft's brig. Vermis, Camille, Elvis and LaFeet looked on from a cell.

"A pig I am. But I'm not stupid! Once we are of no use to you, we're dead anyway." Salurean slapped the former garbage scow skipper.

"I'll make one of you break! I'll find your weakness!" The villain scanned the brig to look at each of the prisoners. He laughed.

"This will be easier than I thought!" He set his gaze on Vermis.

"Get me some petroleum oil. Something from that Karoseum Freighter we hijacked last month! Make sure that it is exactly 38 degrees. Isn't that right my worm friend?"

Vermis began to perspire.

"It is a little warm in here" Salurean taunted. "I am sure that a nice, cool drink would suit you just fine."

Horatio strained at his bonds. "Don't give in! Vermis! Don't"

"You can withstand it", encouraged Camille.

"Yeah", said Elvis. "If I could let them cut my hair" he started. He framed his shaved head to illustrate his point. "You can resist your drinking problem!"

"Um, Um, Um; it is fresh and chilled. Just the way you like it, worm! Would you like a taste?" Vermis began to vibrate visibly.

"Let him out", commanded the pirate leader. His men did so. Salurean brought the cup up to Vermis' lips. A man behind held his head as they forced the oil into his mouth."

"How was that? Don't you want more?"

"Sure" stated Vermis as he stepped back. With one of his concealed setae, he held Salurean's blaster to his head.

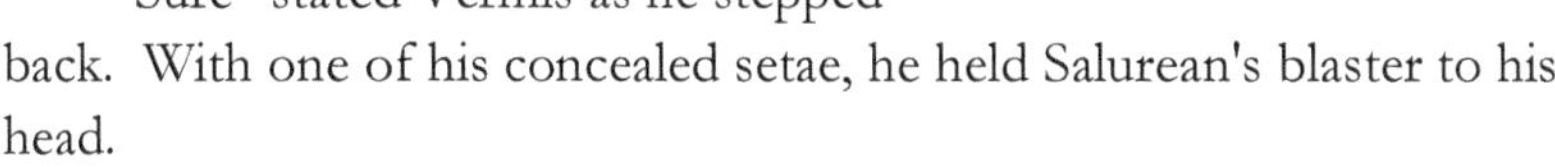

The pirate crew drew their weapons. Salurean cautioned against any activity with his upraised hand

"The key", asked Vermis.

"Give him the key", directed Salurean. Vermis deftly unlocked his handcuffs, and passed the key to Boaracious. Once free, Horatio unlocked the cell. Elvis, Camille and LaFeet each grabbed a weapon from one of the pirates.

"What are you going to do now?" asked Salurean. Vermis looked to La Feet.

"We'll be taking your shuttle, sir. Let's lock them up. Disable the com-link. We should be out of their range before they discover that their friends are in here."

"Why don't you just kill me?"

"Because we are not like you. Not at all! I will live to see you brought to justice! You will face a trial, be found guilty and hung!" stated Vermis. They turned to go, but before they did, Vermis wheeled quickly and grabbed the cup of oil from Salurean's hands.

"Thanks for the drink!" he said. The pirate crew was locked in the brig.

"I'm going to kill that worm!" vowed Salurean. He held a hand up and it dripped slime left from touching Vermis.

Once outside of the detention area, Vermis poured the oil out onto the deck.

"What did you do that for?" asked Elvis.

"I didn't need it anyway!" he stated defiantly.

LaFeet led Horatio and his people to the shuttle bay. The guard was quickly dispatched. They boarded and launched the small craft.

Back at the brig, one of the crew wandered in to see his captain and mates locked up.

"Blast this door, you idiot! Get us out of here!"

The lock gave way to the beam weapon. Salurean quickly ran from the brig, only to slip and fall on the drink poured out by Vermis. Skidding, he slammed against the bulkhead.

"I'm going to kill that worm!" he cursed from the hallway.

"What's eatin' the Captain", asked the pirate who set them free.

"He got a worm under his skin at the moment", explained one of the mates.

"Cap'ns got worms?" the crewman attempted to reason.

The shuttle streaked away from the mother ship.

"We're clear", announced Camille.

"Good. Are there any weapons on this craft?"

"Is this a pirate shuttle, or what?" informed La Feet. "My own it is. She has torpedoes and a nifty warp drive, she has."

"You may have the honors, Jock. Fire one. Then let's warp out of here. Hopefully they will still be disabled when the Outerworld Defense Force gets out here!"

Jock laughed as he pressed the torpedo fire button. The impact and explosion jolted the pirate craft. Before they could return fire, Jock LaFeet's old shuttle had disappeared from the sector.

* * *

Jeremiah Hawks stepped into the Outerworld Defense Force Hall where he was met and embraced by the mayor, Hume DeTosis, of Skyport. While portly, he strolled along side his long time friend with much energy.

"I am afraid that it is far worse than we anticipated, Jeremiah."

"How can that be so, Mayor?"

"Our communications are being blocked."

"If we can't get through to Wakuhn, perhaps we should try Sorttleon or Fawdengi?" asked the professor.

"All of the channels are jammed!"

"That would take a fleet! Such an armada would need to be strategically positioned!"

"For an invasion!" declared the mayor. "I have lost two patrols in the last hour. We were about to call you, when we felt the fusion bomb go off."

"What's been done?"

"All Outerworld Defense Force craft have been drawn to our system to set up a perimeter to repel an invasion. All planetary ODF personnel are at red alert. We will destroy a lot of these Chitins before we end up like LaTruba Two!"

. "Our Alamo", the scientist stated under his breath. He knew that the mayor would not understand his reference nor grasp its significance. "Our Alamo or our Jericho?" echoed a thought. The two came into a control room that was buzzing with activity. Uniformed men and women were stationed at a myriad of monitors and consoles. A high ranking officer gestured to the mayor and Jeremiah Hawks.

"General Kur-Dan", acknowledged the mayor.

"Good, you rescued the professor. We will need you, Jeremiah Hawks. We will need everyone who can hold a blaster, real soon!"

"What do you mean?" asked Hume DeTosis.

"See for yourself." The general motioned to a monitor.

"Horatio Boaracious here", began the video transmission. The former garbage scow skipper stood stoically before the camera. "We engineered an escape from Salurean's pirate ship. We also disabled it. Our intention was to return to Skyport Seven and dispatch the ODF to arrest him.

"Unfortunately, several Chitin Raiders have chased us. We also spied a massive fleet, including several troop transports. Vermis estimates over a million-ground personnel plus support hardware. It is clear to us that Salurean's attack upon our facility has been in concert with this impending invasion. We picked up his distress signal sent to the Chitin fleet.

"We will try to use the superior speed of this shuttle to make contact with the Wakuhnian authorities. In the meantime, it is imperative that you prepare for a full invasion."

May God be with you and with us. Give our best to Professor Hawks."

The transmission ended. There was silence.

"What do you think?" asked the general.

"Hand me a blaster," said the mayor. "Jeremiah Hawks?"

"They rush on the cities, they run on the wall, for great is the army that carries out His Word," recited the professor.

"What is he babbling about, Hume?" asked Kur-Dan.

"I need a quiet place to pray," stated Jeremiah Hawks. "I was recalling a verse that speaks about the judgment of God that came upon a culture on Earth because they did not have faith in Him. This invasion is eerily similar. I need to seek God for His mercy, or Skyport Seven may be overcome!"

"Get a room ready for the Professor!" commanded the general.

"We have a conference room downstairs," volunteered a junior officer.

"You never seemed impressed by the Word of God, General."

"I never needed a miracle before, Professor Hawks. It makes me wonder, that perhaps I have not been living right after all."

At that moment, the room shook under the impact of orbital artillery.

"It's begun!" shouted Kur-Dan. He grabbed a major as he ran by him. "I want every man, woman, child and exotic pet to have a blaster!" he said. "Mayor, please get on the local communications and tell everyone to get into their basement. We will be issuing weapons. Prepare them for the sacrifice that will be required to defend our homes!"

"Yes, General!"

Anti-aircraft guns howled as large objects seemed to fall from the sky and over the horizon.

"What a brazen landing!" commented Kur-Dan. "They must feel that they will overwhelm us!"

"Sir," reported a sergeant, there are too many ships! The landing craft are pouring through and setting down just twenty five clicks from the city."

The general turned to the scientist. "Jeremiah Hawks! Please make me a believer in your God today!" Then he strapped on his sidearm as the professor headed for the room prepared one floor below.

* * *

"Is anything going right?" bellowed Admiral Destrada. Prince Gaius, one of his staff officers, stood in the conference room and patiently listened to his tirade. "The fleet was supposed to deploy yesterday and join us!"

"Sir, the repairs that were called in were necessary. I do not think that we would risk success at LaTruba Two if we left the one Carrier, two Elites and four frigates behind. We have these craft scheduled to rendezvous within the hour."

"Well, this all stinks! I want you to tell me how this God who is in control of the universe can't inspire our Council to fully fund the WDF so our fleet can be ready! Where is your God now, when I need Him the most?"

A junior officer ran into the room. Immediately he panicked when he realized that in his haste he discarded all military protocol. He saluted. His face was a collection of fear induced expressions.

"Will you please stop twitching, son. What is it?"

"Sir, Skyport Seven is under attack! We just received a transmission from Horatio Boaracious and confirmation from a Striker in that sector, that is before his craft was destroyed."

"Sir, we can be at Skyport in a couple of hours!" exclaimed Gaius.

"Give the order to deploy the fleet. Have the stragglers meet us at Skyport." Destrada saluted, and in so doing dismissed the junior officer to relay his orders. The admiral sat down, his countenance a portrait of disbelief. He spoke to the prince.

"Gaius, I am very thankful that I am not in control of the WDF!"

"Sir?"

"I apologize for all that complaining about God. The truth is that we could not be in any better position to assist Skyport Seven. In fact, we should be able to provide a significant element of surprise. If I had planned this, I would be hailed as a military genius! If it were not for all the unexpected interruptions in our deployment, we would be circling LaTruba Two instead of defending Skyport Seven!"

"With all due respect, Admiral, I am not the one to apologize to."

"I know, Gaius. Therefore, before we run off to battle, I want you to pray with me. It is bad enough we have to fight the Chitins. I definitely do not want to continue to be at war with God!"

Chapter Seven: The Shooting Star

Smoke still swirled about the remains of the laboratory. Out of the debris, a head raised.

"Where am I", asked Daria. He was covered with soot, and his body was scorched, as were all of the surroundings within five kilometers.

"I'm alive?" he asked himself. "The last thing I remember I was bleeding all over the place and that there was a fusion mine screeching just before detonation. It sure looks like it went off."

Another voice reverberated in his head.

"The Guardian systems are on line."

"What? I don't have a radio?" Daria smacked his head. Turning to from the shadows, he wiped the black from his legs to reveal the golden sinews of his thighs.

"This is spooky. That's not my leg! Nor is this my leg, or my hand."

"Oracle located!" the annoying voice in his head stated. Reaching down, Daria lifted up the golden embroidered case.

"It's undamaged!" he declared. The shiny backing cast a reflection. The once fallen commander was able to see his image.

As he looked at the reflection, the Guardian seemed to be staring back. He turned to view where he and this being were laying down before the blast.

No one was there.

"Okay. What's going on?"

"Fusion complete" stated the voice within. "Commander Espwin Daria has been fused with Guardian, code name Commander Candle."

Daria looked in disbelief as a shimmering light beamed from his chest. It seemed to be on fire. As he continued to brush himself clean, he found himself to have a golden bronze-like arms and legs with midnight blue trunks and tunic, a golden belt and the florescent yellow candle shining from his chest.

"Why Commander Candle?" he asked

"Your rank remains. A verse of Scripture seems to be implanted in your memory: 'No one hides a candle under a basket but places it where it lights the whole house. Let your light shine so that men may see your good works and give glory to God in heaven"

"Wow. I am the Guardian, or we are."

"I am not an entity or a sentient being. I am the introductory program to assist you in your transition into the calling of a Guardian. I will acquaint you with your new sensory apparatus, how to deploy in combat and tell you how much operational time remains before you need to recharge. I will coach you in every aspect of your mission."

"What is my mission? We have the Oracle! Where's Jeremiah Hawks?" Daria, a.k.a. Commander Candle looked around the ruins. "The shuttle is gone. He would go to Skyport. I guess I could start walking, or even run." Daria looked to a cabinet that seemed to be intact and placed the Oracle within a drawer.

"This should be safe here."

His powerful legs seemed to propel him twenty or thirty feet at a time as he began to build up the velocity of a high-speed monorail.

"I could get used to this."

"It would be more time efficient if you fly"

"I can fly?" No sooner had he asked, and the new guardian found himself rocketing upward, reaching escape velocity. "Yeooooow!" he screamed. His momentum carried him through the hull of a Chitin transport in the middle of its drop toward Skyport Seven.

"What happened?"

"Lesson Number One: You are no longer a mere Wakuhnian!"

The lights clicked on. Daria found himself surrounded by hundreds of husky insects, each towering over him by two or three heads. Several quickly converged upon him, grasping him with sharp claws and some with hands. The commander struck back, his blows breaking through their armor and soaking the floor in their green blood. His experience as a soldier began to overcome his sheer surprise at his new found abilities. He headed to the nose of the craft and disabled the pilot. Flying through the windshield, he depressurized the craft. As he hovered thousands of feet above the planet's surface, he watched the transport drop to the ground and crash.

"That took care of them' he said. He looked around. There were thousands more dropping out of orbit.

"Lesson Number Two: You have enough energy to operate at this level of intensity for five hours."

"Keep the status reports coming every ten minutes," stated the former Striker pilot.

*   *   *

"Sir, I can't explain it! The transports are falling out of the sky!"

"What? What do you mean?"

"Only about ten have landed. The rest are all crashing. I can't explain it!"

"I believe in miracles, I believe in miracles, oh, I believe in miracles!" exclaimed the general.

An infantry officer came into the room and snapped to attention. "What is it Captain?"

"Sir, we can't contain them outside the city. Their commando units have broken through. They are heading right for the ODF command and control center.

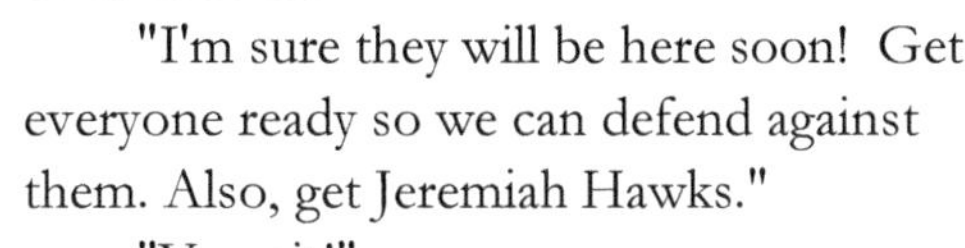

"I'm sure they will be here soon! Get everyone ready so we can defend against them. Also, get Jeremiah Hawks."

"Yes, sir!"

The general reached for a rifle and held it ready for the onslaught.

"Be alert! Keep your weapons ready. Maintain your stations, but be ready to break away into hand to hand combat", he announced.

As if on cue, the sound of buzzing grew closer and closer. A streaking Chitin attempted to fly through the observation glass, only to be squished against it by its own momentum. A rocket blast followed shattering the window. Hundreds of these creatures were crawling up the outer walls. Defense forces fired relentlessly and pushed the clinging attackers down from the window sills. Even more came. The general's weapon was reporting steadily.

The mayor and Jeremiah Hawks found themselves dodging Chitin patrols that had gained access to the ODF building. Floors below the command center, they could hear the battle above them. They were at an impasse. Unable to go upstairs or down, they sought a defensible position on a stairwell. Although each had a pistol, they would not be able to hold off the Chitin's for long.

"It doesn't look good, Jeremiah." the mayor stated.

"From what I have seen, we have been fighting them off in good fashion."

Abruptly the doors below burst open, then those above. Chitins rushed them from both directions.

"Get ready!" Jeremiah cautioned. The weapon in the city official's hand wobbled in fearful anticipation.

"You watch my back, I'll watch yours. We'll fire on three. One, Two…"

A loud weapon report sounded and five Chitins fell from the stairwell. The general stood on the next landing.

"Will you two get up here! We've secured the command center!"

"Go, Mayor!" spoke Jeremiah. He grabbed the politician's gun as Chitin's amassed to rush up the stairs. Both weapons in the professor's hands reported. The mayor was safely inside when Jeremiah Hawks exhausted his energy clips. The marauding insects were upon him quickly, and were prepared to tear him limb from limb. Instead of experiencing the anticipated excruciating death, the scientist found himself slimed with an abundance of these creatures' blood. A golden flash appeared to be striking out at these creatures and driving them back. Dead Chitins were lying all over the place. Jeremiah Hawks caught only glimpses at what he though was his guardian angel. As he sprawled to gain his feet, his mysterious benefactor flew up the staircase and through the skylight on the roof. The professor crawled up the stairs to the command center and slid inside.

"Jeremiah, you're alive!" declared Hume DeTosis.

"Secure that door!" the Kur-Dan yelled. He walked over. He examined the scientist who was saturated with green goop.

"Professor Hawks! Is that you in there?"

"Yes, it is General. Believe me, it smells worse than it looks."

"I believe you! But this day has made me believe in what you stand for. It's been a miraculous day! We've fought them off at every corner and their transports are falling from the sky! Our planetary defenses have held and our fleet has been able to break through their lines. We're not out of the woods, yet, but I never thought we would last this long!"

*   *   *

"Captain Mikko," reported the helmsman, "what is that? It looks like a shooting star!"

"What do you mean a shooting star? It sliced through a frigate? Professor Hawks must have developed a new weapon! Let's support that fire activity! Give me some torpedoes on that ship Ensign!"

"I will be happy to, sir. Three birds away!"

The ODF Captain followed the progress of his missiles. They buried themselves deep into the Chitin craft before ripping it wide open upon detonation. There was a cheer on the cruiser's bridge.

"Follow that shooting star! Load up some more torpedoes!"

"Sir, we have ten raiders on the scope! They are closing fast!"

"Take evasive action! All gunners lock on their targets! We have incoming!"

The sleek raider craft each began firing their particle accelerators, pummeling the ODF cruiser. Their own guns answered back, with only one hit to their credit.

"Sir they are circling! We will not be able to take too much more of this!"

As the raider's completed their maneuver, one, then a second exploded. LaFeet's pirate shuttle streaked through the flash of fallen stunt fighters. It followed in pursuit of a third raider.

"Move into a supporting position! Boys, if they double back on that shuttle, let's make them pay!" yelled the captain.

As La Feet's craft closed in on the third raider, its companions did indeed double back to defend their comrade. The ODF cruiser was ready and riddled the formation with energy blasts. The shuttle followed through by dividing the formation. This allowed the cruiser to dispatch three raiders while the shuttle disabled another. The remaining two Chitin attack ships withdrew to their fleet.

"This is Captain Mikko of the ODF Frigate Enforcer. We appreciate your assistance. Who are you?"

"This is Horatio Boaracious with Jock LaFeet at your service! It was a pleasure Captain Mikko. We appreciate the back-up. Now please set your course for the third moon. The show is about to begin!"

The ODF cruiser followed the shuttle as it banked around the satellite.

"Welcome, Captain Mikko. This is Admiral Destrada, Wakuhnian Defense Force. Please follow point four after the three Elite class cruisers, the Liberty, the Protector and the Royal Crest."

Ahead was the entire Wakuhnian armada. Twenty star ships and fifty five Strikers.

"The Chitin's may have checked in, but they're not checking out!" declared Mikko. "There will be a lot of ships out there so be sure of all targets. Use your computers to identify all energy signatures. Let the big-boys crash the party and we'll make sure no one leaves early."

There was a loud, collective cheer from the crew of The Enforcer.

The Strikers streaked forward to engage the raiders. Scores of dog fights erupted all around the Chitin Cruisers. Then the Wakuhnian star ships moved in. The attacks were well coordinated as each Elite Class Cruiser led a host of war ships selecting Chitin cruisers and frigates one at a time. The enemy ships were individually blown apart in quick succession by the concentrated fire.

On the bridge of the Protector, Admiral Destrada directed the movements of his fleet. "Frigates twenty two through thirty one, give me more fire support on the enemy cruiser in sector four! Keep your marks between yourself and the planet! Royal Crest! You are leaving your escorts behind. Tighten up that formation! Liberty, what's going on? Ensign! Tell me what that is? It's streaking into the engineering sections of the Chitin cruisers!"

"I don't know, sir! The other ships are reporting the phenomena, but we have no explanation! Whatever it is, it has disabled over twenty ships!"

"Let's focus on the ones that are fully operational. We'll come back to finish these later!"

* * *

"Horatio!" called a voice on the shuttle’s communication system, "This is Captain Mikko. Destrada wants you to lead me and two other ODF frigates to Salurean's ship. It looks like everything is under control in this sector. They do not need us!"

"That is good news, Captain Mikko," answered the pleased porker, “Follow my lead. They may have some fighter support, so we'll handle the small craft. Have the frigates flank you as you move in."

"That's a plan, Horatio.

La Feet directed Vermis on the course and the formation as the star craft sped toward Salurean's last position.

"Do you think we'll get him, Jock?"

"We hit him pretty hard, but he's a scurvy devil. If he has any engines he's moving."

"I'm on the scanners" stated Elvis as he jumped into a seat at a bridge station. "I'll look for debris and any ion particle clusters."

"You have a good crew, Horatio. They run themselves. Who's your best gunner?"

"I am," stated Camille. "I'll set our lasers for the small craft."

"I'll man the torpedoes, Jock", volunteered Boaracious. He paused thoughtfully at his station. "Do you think we will take him alive?" he asked.

"No", said LaFeet cryptically. "Not if I have anything to say about it!"

Fifty Chitin Raiders were suddenly upon the shuttle, cruiser and two frigates.

"Fly through them, Vermis!" commanded Jock La Feet. "They'll be after the larger craft. We'll let the big ships handle them. Let's get Salurean!"

Camille made her laser blasts count and three raiders were hit. This caused the formation coming at them to disperse and gave Captain Mikko and his frigates more inviting targets than if the stunt fighters remained on course. Mikko left the other ships to handle the raiders while he followed La Feet's shuttle.

A group of Chitin corvettes encircled Salurean's pirate ship. Immediately the battle was on as Vermis banked wildly to the left and then to the right to avoid ray fire. While Mikko's cruiser was taking hits, his own weapon batteries began to silence the corvettes one by one.

"We need to break off" stated Elvis suddenly.

"What do you mean?" asked La Feet. "Trust him Jock!" cried Boaracious.

"Hard to port, and fly her apart if you have to!" shouted LaFeet.

Salurean's pirate craft exploded. It seemed to ignite all of the corvettes, which followed in succession. Mikko tried to guide his cruiser away from the blasts, but his command was caught in the explosion's wake. While the craft remained intact, it listed as it sat motionless.

"How did you know?" questioned La Feet.

"The energy reading on my sensors ascended rapidly, and that usually indicates a self-destruct sequence."

"Was there anyone on board?" asked Horatio.

"Everyone! He blew up fifty of his own crew and the personnel on the corvettes."

"I guess he wasn't going to be taken alive" observed Vermis.

"He's alive" stated Horatio who moved over to Elvis' station. "I have a warp signature moving away from the pirate ship."

"The escape pod" informed La Feet with much resignation. "Let's hail Mikko and see how we can help out," Jock started. "Then call in the frigates. We'll have a lot of casualties, but it was a miracle his ship held together."

"What about pursuing the escape pod?"

"I'm sure Salurean is heading to a very secure location", stated Boaracious. "It would be too much of a risk, and the vessels damaged in the battle and their crews need our attention now."

*   *   *

Blasters were raised up high. The mayor and the general were walking down the central square. Residents were coming up to them amid numerous congratulations and a lot of hand shaking going on. Dead Chitins were everywhere. Children were playing with dismembered pincers, causing them to open and close.

Jeremiah Hawks looked to the horizon. Skyport's setting sun highlighted the hills, behind which lie the professor's destroyed residence and laboratory. He wondered about Daria, assuming that his new found friend did not survive the assault. He also mused over the many people he lost including his wife, his children, Manta, Joktar and Ted Collins. He was hoping to hear from Horatio, Vermis, Camille and Elvis. It was heartening that they escaped from Salurean. Clearly they reached Wakuhn to mobilize their fleet. Hopefully, they would be landing soon.

The scientist thought about this character, Salurean. Why was he after him and his motley crew of entrepreneurs? Was it his support of the Wakuhnians? Or did he have it in for Earthmen? If this was the case, Jeremiah Hawks could only guess at the fate of Ted Collins.

"Jeremiah", called the mayor. He placed his hand upon the earthman's shoulder.

"Your friends will be landing their sloop soon. They will be at port forty six."

"Thank you Hume."

"What is that?" the politician said as he pointed to the sky. "It must be falling debris that is burning up."

"It is heading for where my laboratory used to be!" said the scientist thoughtfully. "I better check it out! Please have Horatio and the others meet me."

"It's almost night time, Jeremiah. What do you hope to do? It will be dark soon! I would look at the crash site in the morning."

"It may be too late!"

The professor ran to his shuttle port and found his vehicle undamaged from the siege. Soon he was airborne and trying to beat the onset of night. As he hovered over the hills between his old residence and the city, he turned his landing lights on. He put the shuttle down within yards of the blast damage to his laboratory.

There in the midst of the destruction was a fresh crater! The scientist ran to its side and looked down.

It was the Guardian!

"You were activated! It was you knocking the transports down!" Jeremiah Hawks carefully climbed down the crater's side to the Guardian below.

"Design limits exceeded", spoke the Guardian. "System shut down imminent."

"I need Nultron energy, but how?"

"Professor?" called a voice from above. "Are you down there?"

"Vermis? How did you get here?"

"The Mayor told us that you were heading for the laboratory, or what is left of it. I took a drop pack from the sloop. Horatio and the rest are on their way."

"Please climb down here!" implored Jeremiah Hawks. "It's the Guardian! He needs our help!"

Unexpectedly, the worm's head popped out of the ground next to the professor.

"Yeoow! You scared me! What are you doing?"

"I'm a worm, Professor! This is easier on me than climbing down."

"The Guardian came to life! He needs Nultron energy!"

"We have a reactor on the company freighter, the Terra-Quest. We're docked on the fourth moon. It didn't see any action today, so it should be in good shape. I'll call Captain Tinlisp and tell him to get her underway."

"Excellent! We have to get the Guardian up there, fast!"

Chapter Eight: Counterplot!

"The ODF and Wakuhnian Empire have agreed to cooperate with each other to retake LaTruba Two." reported Horatio. The professor was reviewing a report when his chief of staff entered the make-shift laboratory aboard the freighter Terra-Quest.

"What's the plan?" asked Jeremiah Hawks as he looked up from his work.

"The fleets will be gathering at Fawdengi. They will begin the blockade and then commence an orbital bombardment. Three days later the landings will begin."

"What do they need from us?"

"They desire LaFeet and his shuttle as an advance scout. Camille and Elvis have an opportunity to be officers on the Royal Crest. Vermis has received a commission as bridge officers on ODF cruiser. They did wish to speak with you before they accept."

The scientist rose and smiled.

"I appreciate their loyalty. Imagine how far we've come! I am thrilled to see each of you receive this new respect. What about you, Horatio?"

“I could have my own cruiser, but I feel my place is here with you Professor. There is still a lot of work to do on the home front. A successful invasion of LaTruba Two will not be the end of this ugly business with the Chitins."

Jeremiah Hawks turned to his longtime friend. "I’m glad you're staying, Horatio."

"Also, General Kur-Dan asked for prayer for the plans and the forces carrying out the attack."

"I would not expect anything less from our friend the General."

"Any developments from the Guardian?" asked Horatio. The professor led the chief of staff into a second room.

"Yes and no. I believe that the Nultron field has stabilized his systems. I am not sure he is "charging up" so to speak. In fact, I’m frustrated that I am unable to understand how he even works.

“It was a long time before he became active. What energized him up this time?" asked Boaracious.

"I am not sure. I suspect that it was the fusion mine detonation. But it was such a random event. I do not believe we can duplicate all the necessary parameters. There may be another explanation for the activation."

"It has only been a couple of weeks," Horatio stated with a sense of optimism. "Perhaps he will come back into operation sooner this time?"

"I sure hope so. I really hope he does."

The two looked up at the Guardian who was suspended within a Nultron field inside of the transparent bell housing.

"Maybe he is an angel," speculated Horatio.

"That was my first thought, but I don't think so. Angels are truly celestial beings, spirits, and they do not hang around in a comatose state after their work is done. This is definitely a robot, but I still cannot discern even the simplest of energy transfer circuits." The professor picked up small wafer like items from a nearby barrel.

"They are nothing like these silicon units. When I was on Earth we were using vacuum tubes and our appliances were larger as a result. With the way we were developing computer technology, I would not be surprised if these units; what did you call them?"

"Chips" informed Boaracious.

"I would not be surprised if our scientist were working on these. But the Guardian is entirely different! There are no chips or circuitry, no gears, joints or any such structural exoskeleton! He is a mass of very dense, lightweight and fluid metal. I can't even tell you why he maintains his present shape."

"Perhaps we are not supposed to know, Professor. Maybe he is our miracle, a one of a kind happening for our benefit. Maybe there is no scientific explanation."

The scientist placed his clipboard down and laughed.

"You're right! I'm here to minister the Word of God! I keep being a scientist first. Am I really this much of a workaholic?"

Before Horatio could confirm the professor's assertion, a communication panel sounded to indicate an incoming call. The scientist and Horatio moved to see who was on line.

"Mayor?' hailed Jeremiah. "How is the rebuilding going?"

"Jeremiah Hawks! It is good to see you! The rebuilding is proceeding rapidly! We have restored power and communications. The damage to the buildings will take longer, but no one has to spend the night on the street."

"Excellent! Horatio and I have been working on a plan to speed up these repairs as well. I am convinced that we can be back to normal within a couple of months."

"I have no doubt. But I did have another reason to call on you. I want you to be my guest at dinner tonight. I have a special visitor and he has insisted on seeing you."

"Who is visiting Skyport?"

"Prince Gaius, King Zilgasser of Wakuhn's brother. He is the first officer of the Protector of the Realm."

"Horatio and I will shuttle down within the hour, Mayor."

"Splendid! You have been working very hard. I look forward to seeing you!" The screen became blank as the transmission ended.

"I have been obsessed with work again, eh, Horatio?"

"Yes, boss. It's been three weeks since we repelled the Chitins, and you haven't taken a break from trying to awaken the Guardian."

"I must be a workaholic!"

"No," Boaracious disagreed, "more like a compulsive work-a-holic."

"I'm even doing a poor job of that, too. Let's get the shuttle fired up Horatio. Mayor Hume DeTosis will serve up a grand buffet. You'll have to bring your appetite."

"I'm a Porker, Professor. Our species' middle name is 'appetite'."

* * *

It was dark. Daria felt chilled to the bone. It was a struggle to open his eyes. There was a sound of lab equipment and monitors all around, but he heard these faintly, as if they were distant.

"What's going on?" asked the commander.

"System's are still off line. You exceeded operational limits."

"We are not charging up fast enough. I feel so sluggish."

"Commander Candle unit requires more than artificial light."

"The Nultron field hold is keeping us alive, but we need an energy source!"

"'Us" is not an appropriate adjective. I am not an entity. I am an instructional program. Soon, I will end all instructional recordings."

"I have to get word to the professor somehow. He probably thinks I'm dead! How can I charge myself up? What are the acceptable energy sources and how do I access them?"

"These are solar, electrical, and heat. These energy sources are absorbed through your outer surface."

"Then, all I have to do is to get out of the Nultron field unit and access a significant power source."

"That is correct. However, you may risk a total shut down. You must access power quickly!"

Daria pressed against the glass that held him inside. Drawing back a fist, he flung it forward and cracked it. A second blow shattered the barrier, and he fell to the deck. Slowly, he crawled to the nearest monitor. He stretched to reach the power coupling that energized the unit.

"I don't know if I can make it!" he groaned.

"Instructional programming shutting down"

Commander Candle slumped to the metal deck.

* * *

"I am Prince Gaius, the King's younger brother", announced the Wakuhnian by the mayor's side. Hume DeTosis beamed with civic pride. This was his first opportunity to entertain anyone of royal blood.

"Jeremiah Hawks" replied the professor as he bowed politely, "and this is my chief operating officer, Horatio Boaracious." Horatio bowed to the prince.

"Please, there is no need to be so formal. I am honored to be received by the mayor and to meet with you. I am not here as a royal representative, but as the new first officer of the Protecto*r*. Each of you has performed a great service for the Outerworlds and the Empire. While I cannot speak for my brother officially, I know that he is eagerly awaiting your arrival on Wakuhn."

"I look forward to that time as well, Prince Gaius. We have appreciated your work on behalf of the Zinj political prisoners. This has been accomplished at quite a personal cost. If you supported the status quo, I am sure you would be enjoying a cabinet position by now."

"My military career and subordinate position assist me in easing any insecurity my brother may have about my political agenda. Those who do not want change try to cite personal ambition on my part. I am happy to demonstrate that this is not the case."

The mayor motioned for everyone to gather at the table. As they sat down, a Wakuhnian ensign approached the prince and whispered something to him.

"Gentlemen, I have surprising news. A shuttle is on its way. An envoy from my brother will be joining us later today."

"Very good!" stated the mayor. "It promises to be a very special week. Shall we begin tonight's banquet?"

"Music to an old boar's ears" laughed Horatio for the professor's hearing only.

* * *

"What's the mission, Elvis?" prodded Camille as they walked briskly through the under deck of the Protector. They were coming up to the carrier section of the cruiser.

"We're taking a Striker Supreme to pick up a possible intelligence source, an informant who managed to escape from LaTruba Two."

"I'm going to fly a Striker?" asked Camille.

"Shhhhh!' cautioned Elvis. "They think I can fly one. And don't tell anyone anything different or the mission will be scrubbed. Wakuhnians are very particular about who they let fly these babies."

Camille kissed Elvis on the cheek. His blue skin immediately turned red.

"What did you do that for?"

"Now I know that you care for me!"

Elvis didn't have an answer for his partner's assertion. Very quickly they were strapped in to the adjoining seats in the cockpit and the extra large fighter was propelled into space.

* * *

La Feet sat in his command chair, patiently observing a new schooner class craft from within the shadow of an asteroid.

"Look at those lines, Jimmy" he said as he leaned toward his executive officer. "She's beautiful, but she wasn't designed by anyone we know. We need to keep an eye on her, but be sure she doesn't have an eye out for us."

"Sir, I am confident that we have evaded any sensor scan" informed the first mate.

"Aye, and we have, or else she would have turned on us by now. If it's Salurean's ship, he's up to no good! We're going to set here a spell and see what this snake is up to."

"I will minimize our energy signature, sir. The magnetic field of this asteroid should mask our own sensor surveillance."

"That's why I went and got you, Jimmy boy! I am very obliged that you and the crew came when I called."

"It is part of our repentance from dead works, boss. Who would think that we could be the "good guys?"

"It is good to be on the right side of the law, let alone an arm of the law! Let's keep in the shadows, too, so they don't get a visual on us either."

"Yes, sir; hopefully we will get to put Salurean away."

LaFeet scratched his head thoughtfully.

"Kur-Dan, you wanted some intelligence on Salurean. I think you may have it! I really stunk as a pirate! But I'm making one heck of a marshal!"

* * *

The evening went well and the mayor was very pleased with his staff and their efforts to make the prince feel welcome. After the banquet, Jeremiah Hawks and Gaius were walking along the observation deck of Skyport's city center.

"Finally, we can speak" Gaius said, relieved.

"Well, we aren't supposed to know each other. Tell me, has Manta been set free?"

"Not yet. My brother is perturbing me by stalling the releases. There is a lot of pressure on him from the council to maintain the status quo."

"Separafytes?"

"No, at least they cannot be identified as such."

"But who is stalling the process?"

"This past year an Outerworlder named Snillosh has been awarded a seat on the Interplanetary Council. He made his money on using LaTruba

Two as a main port to sell food and technology to the Chitins. Once LaTruba Two was taken, he became the beneficiary of a lot of sympathy. He's really cashed in on it, too. I am afraid that he is having an undue influence on my brother."

"Snillosh? None of my lobbyists have been given any time to see him."

"Nor have I until recently. My young nephew Arisue informed me of his frequent visits with his father, the king."

"I'm concerned, Gaius. The attack on Skyport was too well planned. I am convinced that the Chitins and Salurean had inside information about our defenses and my laboratory."

"I am concerned, as well. And that is really why I am here. I need your help to discover if my brother is being coerced or compromised. Your upcoming visit is very important."

"So important, I can anticipate another effort to keep me away from my meeting with him on Wakuhn!"

"Precisely, but I was under the impression that my brother sent a body guard to protect you on your trip?"

"He did. He sent Commander Espwin Daria."

"Daria? Yes, the commander saved my brother from an assassination attempt. I also have spent some time with him. He was very eager to meet with you. He is a believer, for sure! I never had a more grateful guest, as the day I gave him one of the Bibles you publish. Is he on another assignment?"

"No, Prince Gaius, he perished during the attack. He protected my flight from Salurean's men and was in my laboratory when the fusion mine detonated."

"I am so sorry, Jeremiah. There was not a better Wakuhnian in the galaxy! He gave his life to see that you were safe. I shall inform my brother. He shall receive every honor and we shall make provision for his family."

"That would be appreciated very much, Prince Gaius."

* * *

It hit the Terra-Quest with the force of a torpedo.

"Tinslisp here, what was that?" called the ship's captain. He was on an auxiliary deck and was seeking information from the bridge.

"I don't know!" cried the bridge officer. "The hull's been breached by some kind of projectile. There hasn't been an explosion. I am sending a damage control team to Deck Twelve."

"That's where the professor's laboratory is located!"

The freighter listed under the impact. The damage control team rushed to energize a containment field to maintain atmospheric pressure in the affected compartments. The men turned as they heard loud clanging against the metal deck approach their location.

It sounded like footsteps! Abruptly, it burst through a cargo hold door, penetrating and twisting the thick metal. The metal construct was huge, over three meters tall! It had massive thick metallic arms and legs that were powerfully build into a stocky body.

"A Death Droid!" exclaimed the frightened damage control officer. "I've heard about these things! They have been showing up to abduct dignitaries so the pirates can ransom them."

"And assassinate law enforcement in the Outerworlds," commented another.

They drew their weapons and fired. The blasts ricocheted off the robot. "We need bigger guns! Let's get out of here!"

The damage control party fled. The Death Droid marched relentlessly toward Jeremiah Hawk's laboratory. It crashed through the door, the sound of shredding metal echoing through the freighter's corridors. The automaton engaged a motion detector from its chest and began to direct it in a sweep of the laboratory. The darkened lab's secrets were scanned as it passed from side to side slowly.

At that moment the overhead lamps flickered on. The first object visible was the bell housing. It was shattered and empty. The Death Droid turned its attention elsewhere, continuing to scan the room.

His interest was drawn to Commander Candle, who was standing by an equipment terminal. He had a power coupling attached to his chest.

"Looking for me, big fella?" he asked.

The robot rushed toward Daria. The guardian jumped as the mechanical menace plowed through the freighter's wall. Quickly, Commander Candle affixed the cable to make contact with the robot's head. Electrical power coursed through the metal monster's body. It vibrated wildly.

The Death Droid rolled forward until it reached the cable's length and it broke free from the strong electrical current.

"You will need to do more than that to destroy me!" spoke the construct.

"Perhaps you can deliver a message to your master Salurean."

"What message?"

"This!"

The commander flew like a bullet into the Death Droid's midsection. Both crashed through wall after wall before coming to a tumbling stop inside a large cargo hold. Daria followed his advantage by delivering a crushing right and left. Metal pieces flew from the robot with each impact.

The Death Droid launched a missile that appeared from inside his wrist. Commander Candle evaded the projectile. It punched a hole through the outer frame of the freighter.

"Hull breach!" announced a voice over the Terra-Quest "comlink", "We cannot seal it! All hands abandon ship!" Unmoved by the commotion, the Death Droid lunged at Commander Candle.

Daria rolled beneath the hulk to strike the massive robot from behind. It sprawled forward toward the opening in the hull. The vacuum of space began to pull at the robot.

"I hope that did it!" spoke Daria to himself, "I managed to charge up a little, but I really need more time. Hmmm," he said thoughtfully, "maybe there is a way for me to but more time?"

The metallic creation struggled forward.

"I am here to take you back to Salurean", informed the robot. "He will be your new programmer."

"I am not his to program, nor will I permit you to carry out yours!"

Moving with surprising speed, the Death Droid landed a right cross. Commander Candle was thrown backward into a control panel. As it shattered, electricity arched upward into the guardian's body. When the smoke settled, Daria lie still.

"Now you are mine" the Death Droid stated. It lifted Commander Candle's motionless form and flew through the opening in the Terra-Quest's hull and into outer space.

Chapter Nine: Blast from the Past

Elvis and Camille cautiously walked through the caverns. Their pistols were raised against any threat. Elvis carried a lantern in his other hand and was shining it toward every nook and onto the path ahead.

"This way called a voice."

The two followed it into a small room. Inside sat a rather pathetic looking creature. Humanoid in appearance, the flesh seemed to be melded into a wide android's body. He was truly half man and half machine.

"Who are you?" Camille asked.

"Allow me to introduce myself," the stranger spoke. He turned to Elvis and Camille. His face was a chaotic mix of circuitry, exposed wires and skin.

"I am Alexander Tweed. I am the third person from Earth into this sector of space. When I was sent here the teleportation beam fused me with a mining drone on LaTruba Two. I know everything about the Chitin's defenses, so it is imperative that I am taken to your military authorities for a debriefing. After that, I would like to be taken to see Jeremiah Hawks."

"That is the plan," stated Elvis. "Do you know what happened to the people of LaTruba Two?"

"Yes and no. I know that they were taken away. Where and for what, I cannot tell you. I was left behind since they were convinced that I was just a mining drone."

"Let's get going then'" Camille suggested.

"Please. I am ailing. My biggest fear is that I do not have much time left. That is why I must see Jeremiah Hawks."

Camille and Elvis assisted Alexander Tweed, or what was left of him through the catacombs and out to their Striker Supreme. Moments later, the craft lifted off and sped to Skyport Seven with their newest intelligence asset.

* * *

Prince Gaius ran up to Jeremiah Hawks.

"Your freighter is under attack. Come with me on my shuttle to the Protector. You will be safe there."

Horatio nodded his assent to encourage the professor. "Let's go!"

"Thank you Gaius."

They began to walk quickly through the shuttle terminal.

"I have arranged for envoy Snillosh to meet with us there. I also have a survivor from LaTruba Two on his way as well. We want to debrief him. He wants to meet with you. According to Elvis and Camille, he's from Earth, also."

"Who could that be?"

"His name is Alexander Tweed."

Jeremiah stopped and stood still. "Tweed!" he uttered angrily.

"You know him?" Horatio asked.

"Yes. He's the one responsible for me being here. I was his captive on Earth. I am also convinced that he sent one of his agents to try to kill my family."

"Then he may not be a reliable source," Gaius observed.

"That, my friend, would be an understatement!"

The three continued their route through the terminal to the prince's shuttle.

"What are you going to do when you see him, boss?" Horatio asked.

"Hopefully, I will be able to control myself, old friend. I have enjoyed a great sense of peace these past years. Just the mere mention of the name "Tweed" stirs up a torrent in my soul. I hope to God I can actually forgive him. But knowing him, I can't help but suspect that he is a major player in this dark drama. He is the only person I know who has been given over to evil so much so..."

"He could be Salurean!" Horatio completed the thought.

* * *

"What's that!?" asked LaFeet as he pointed to a small shuttle leaving Salurean's pirate craft. "Get a sensor lock, Jimmy boy!"

"I will sir!"

There was silence for a couple of seconds. "What is it lad?"

"Good news and bad news sir."

"Yer talkin' in riddles! Give it to me plain!"

"I have a positive ID. It is a Wakuhnian transport."

"The plot thickens! So what's the bad news?"

La Feet's craft suddenly rocked leeward.

"We've been discovered!"

"Take evasive action! Let's send a missile their way. We need to get this information back to General Kur-Dan!"

La Feet's ship sped up to maximum impulse as the star schooner fired upon it.

"Calculate a course! Let's get to warp speed boys, now!" The craft lurched from a hit.

"Warp's gone, sir" informed Jimmy.

"Let's make a run." instructed the captain.

"I don't get it? They are not pursuing us!" Jimmy exclaimed.

"There's your answer!" informed LaFeet.

Ahead were hundreds of Chitin raiders and fifty transports.

"If you don't succeed, try and try again!" exclaimed the former privateer. "They're doing an end around while we tighten up the blockade at LaTruba Two. After all, Skyport Seven is more important!"

"There are twenty bogies coming in!"

"Let's go down fighting! Battle stations!" commanded LaFeet.

* * *

The Protector was at full alert. Strikers were dispatched to rescue the crew of the severely damaged Terra-Quest. Shuttles joined the search party. Sensors were used to locate every object drifting from the freighter. Jeremiah Hawks was on the bridge with Prince Gaius. His eyes flashed through the sensor logs hoping that all hands would be accounted for. He was also trying to locate any sign of the Guardian.

"Admiral on the bridge" announced Gaius. A distinguished Wakuhnian officer strode confidently to his command chair.

"What caused all of this damage?" he asked.

"The survivors we've picked up believe that the freighter was attacked by a Death Droid, sir"

"One of Salurean's mechanical assassins? We have experienced their sabotage before! I have no doubt that he was after you, Professor."

"Or they were after the Guardian, Captain?"

"Actually, I am Admiral Destrada. I am honored to have you aboard the Protector, Professor. My instincts tell me that we have not seen any end to the attacks upon your person and property. I am sending a squadron of Strikers to track down that Death Droid."

"I would not advise that," interrupted Horatio Boaracious.

"A Porker correcting a Wakuhnian Admiral?" spoke Destrada sarcastically.

"Horatio?" added Jeremiah Hawks. He was embarrassed by his chief of staff's abruptness.

"Do not worry Professor," spoke Destrada, "Horatio and I go back a long time. I know he's on to something."

The admiral stood from his command chair. "We will be in the war room. Keep the reports coming! Gaius, you're with me. Number three, you have the bridge. Stay at red alert. I want to rescue all of the Terra-Quest crew!"

The fleet officer paused as he led his guests off the bridge.

"Tell me when the informer arrives and when envoy Snillosh gets here. Have him sent to the officer's conference suite to wait for me."

"Yes sir!"

Destrada, the prince, professor and a porker retired to a room adjacent to the bridge.

* * *

LaFeet's boldness caught the Chitins by surprise. He was able to disable three raiders very quickly. This bought time to strategize. He popped up a star chart on the pilot's overhead display.

"Jimmy, chart a course for here," he spoke as he pointed on the map.

"But sir, this will take us away from Skyport!"

"Yes it will, my boy. But it is our job to stay alive, long enough to get a message to the fleet. These scurvy devils will draw a hard line between us and Skyport, but I bet that their rear flank is softer. Our torpedo count is low, so we need a place to hide. We're real close, so if we can make a break for the asteroid Yargo, there are some mining shafts there."

"But even if we make it, we could be bottled up for days! It could be too late for Skyport!"

"Yes sir, Jimmy! But being bottled up isn't so bad, if you know the person who owns the bottle!"

"Now you are talking in riddles, sir!"

"Just fly her Jimmy, boy! There!"

La Feet pointed to a large cavern in the side of an asteroid. As they approached, about twenty Chitin Raiders closed in for the kill.

Quite unexpectedly, dozens of gun turrets appeared out of the crust of this planetoid. The assault of unleashed ray fire vaporized the attacking craft almost instantly.

"Did you see that? Did you see that!" exclaimed Jimmy.

"I sure did, but I bet they didn't! I was counting on the defenses to recognize that we were being pursued. Take her in and dock at the first bay ya see."

The shuttle moved within a rugged spaceport. A huge craft flanked them on the port side as they came about to a lit docking area.

"What is this place?" asked Jimmy

"It used to be my home away from home", answered LaFeet. "All stop. Let's drift to our docking position. Now hold!"

The shuttle lurched slightly. La Feet and the bridge crew had braced themselves in anticipation.

"We're in! Let's go lads. Let's get to the air lock."

They walked through a short corridor where a line-up at the doorway ensued.

"You look a little nervous, Captain La Feet", observed Jimmy.

"Yeah, I haven't been back for a while. I'm not sure if my old man is here. And if he is..."

The door whooshed open. An ancient, scrawny version of Jock La Feet, complete with the characteristic large appendages, stood alone.

"Where the heck is my idiot son!" he bellowed. “Only he is stupid enough to lead a squadron of stunt fighters here!”

"He'll be quite angry," explained LaFeet.

The old man walked through the crew, his eyes straining to recognize a face. Jock was flinching as his father approached. The old man grabbed him by the ear, and smacked him on the head.

"Twenty years! You come back after twenty years! On top of everything else you bring a fool navy after ya, too! My sensors are over heating! There are thousands of ships out there!"

"Take it easy Pappy! Take it easy!"

"So which side are ya on, and who's after ya?" asked Pappy. He released his grip on his estranged son. La Feet's crew quietly chuckled as they watched their commander being humiliated by his father. "And where did you get that good looking ship! You're darn lucky that I know how you fly, or I would have toasted you too!"

"I'm with the Wakuhnians, Pappy"

Like lightning the elder La Feet grabbed his son's ear, and smacked him again.

"Are you an utter moron? Did you lead them here? Don't you know I'm a wanted man?"

"That must run in the family", observed Jimmy.

Pappy released his grip. Jock's ear was red, and not insignificantly, stretched out.

"What do you mean?"

"Jock was a fierce pirate, wanted by the Outerworlds and Wakuhn alike. But when the whole sector was invaded by an alien race, Captain La Feet turned the tide of the battle with timely intelligence and intrepid leadership. He won a pardon for himself. Those of us from his old crew, who were discarded by Salurean, joined Captain LaFeet in his new command."

Pappy was stunned.

"My idiot son is a hero?"

"The very backbone of the new alliance between the Outerworlds and Wakuhn!" clarified Jimmy.

Still in a daze, Pappy affectionately patted his son's shoulder. "A La Feet finally amounted to something." As his father turned to lead the men off the shuttle, Jock handed Jimmy a gold coin.

"You're never one to miss an opportunity, eh Jimmy? Thanks for saving my ear!"

"Then there's a battle raging outside?" asked the elder LaFeet.

"Yes, there is Pappy. That's why we're here. We are behind the enemy lines, but need some fire power to break through and warn the Alliance. Chitin ships have massed against Skyport Seven just as the Alliance fleet has been dispatched to liberate LaTruba Two."

"Aye, that would be a very bad trade-off. I never liked LaTruba Two. It is dusty and too hot!"

"What do you have that can help?" asked Jock.

"Wait a minute! What's in it for me?"

The spy shuttle captain and former pirate scourge replied with a blank expression. He looked Jimmy's way for some help.

"How does a full pardon sound, Mr. LaFeet! Jock's commission allows him to offer that for your assistance."

Pappy turned away to consider the proposal. Jock handed Jimmy another gold coin.

"I won't have to hide anymore?"

"No, Pappy. You'll be free!"

"Yihaaa!" celebrated the elder La Feet. "If that's the case, son, take my dreadnaught, the Whirlwind! I've been working on it for twenty years. She's got some speed, but also a lot of firepower. I guarantee that you'll do some damage!"

"Can we run her with a crew of five?"

"Fully automated"

"Does she have torpedoes?"

"I only had a hundred and twenty. There's room for thirty more!" stated Pappy with pride.

"Are you coming with us?" asked Jock.

"Naw, I'm not leaving until I see the pardon. Besides, my base defenses may come in handy. You can lure some more of those stunt fighters so I can grease them!"

"What about communicating with Skyport Seven?"

"They are probably jammed. But we can get a message through to Luna One. Then get my defenses primed to handle the heat!"

"It's a plan!" announced Jock. "Jimmy, take the boys and warm up the dreadnaught. Transfer our three torpedoes from the shuttle. I'll get word to Luna One and help Pappy get all of his defenses on line."

"Aye aye, sir!"

"This way sonny!" stated his father as he pointed down a corridor.

"Please give me a moment, Pappy. I have to speak with my XO!" He turned to Jimmy.

"Good thinking. I'll be a poor man, but you managed to get my Pappy going in the right direction."

"What was he wanted for?"

"Nothing, my mom was so stressed having him around, she had him served with a false warrant! I never had the heart to tell him!"

"Where's your mother?"

"She is at home! She's too stubborn to tell him it was all a joke!"

"It look's like your family has a communication problem", observed Jimmy.

"And that's why you still have an income. Call it job security. Now get that dreadnaught up and ready!"

* * *

Gauis walked into the cell block first. The guard acknowledged him. Camille and Elvis flanked the dying Alexander Tweed, who was being attended by a physician. Gaius waved to Professor Hawks and he entered the room.

As he saw the professor, Tweed lunged forward. But instead of assaulting him, as feared, he fell grasping his feet.

"Thank God!" he sobbed. "Thank the Lord!"

"Tweed!" called the professor, somewhat crossly.

"Jeremiah!, you have every right to be angry with me! Please, hear me out! I'm dying!"

"I'm here."

"I have sinned against God and you, so grievously that even this fusion with a mining droid does not even begin to equate with the punishment I deserve! I beg you for your forgiveness, Jeremiah Hawks."

"Why should I believe you, Tweed? How do I know you are not misleading me, as you did once before?" asked the professor.

"I understand your skepticism. I don't blame you. Please hear me out. I followed you and Collins into the beam" Tweed began his narrative, "but the telemetry was off. I ended up on LaTruba Two, merged with this robot. The first couple of months I found myself disoriented and confused from a maddening collection of my own memories and a mining program. In the recesses of my mind, I recalled a Sunday school lesson about King Nebuchadnezzar; how he lost his mind for seven years because of his pride. I found myself begging God to have my mind back.

"One day my thoughts cleared. I discovered that with out the distractions I occupied myself with on Earth, my soul became exceedingly still. And that's when I discovered how easy it was to sense the presence of God and meditate upon His word. I heard His call on my life, and surrendered to Him! Bible verses I tried so hard to forget became fresh and new to me. I purposed to fulfill my days however God chose

“My first opportunity for ministry occurred on LaTruba Two. There I was ignored as a lowly mining drone. However, it gave me opportunity to help Zinj and other slaves to escape to freedom!

“It allowed me to over hear conspirators who were bribed to disable the early warning network that guarded LaTruba Two. I escaped with the next group of slaves and was granted passage to the Negli asteroids. There I could remain undetected with other mining drones. It was from there I made contact with the Empire when I heard of the attack upon Skyport. Elvis and Camille finally picked me up so I could stand before you.

“Now my cybernetic interface has been shutting down systems and I fear that my days are few. In addition to the intelligence I have, all I want to do is ask your forgiveness Jeremiah Hawks, as I know God would have me do. Please, I ask you again, can you forgive me for all the evil I have done to you?"

The scientist stood motionless as the tears flowed from the half man half machine prostrate before him.

"I forgive you in the name of Jesus Christ, Alexander. And I ask you to serve him with whatever time you may have to live."

"Thank you. I can die in peace now."

Jeremiah Hawks lifted up the man who destroyed his life on Earth. “There is no time for that. We need you to live for Him."

Destrada stepped into the room.

"I see you have spoken our survivor from LaTruba Two. Is he ready to help us with the information we need?"

"I am" said Tweed. "Let me start with the information I gained prior to the Chitin invasion of LaTruba Two. First of all, it was clear that our defenses were compromised by the work of a traitor! And while I recognized him, he did not know who I was."

* * *

The Death Droid entered Salurean's craft via the shuttle bay. "I have the robot created by Jeremiah Hawks," it stated.

"What about the Professor?" asked a short creature with a pale complexion. He had large lash-less eyes and petite ears. His head was rather large compared to his body.

"He was not on the freighter"

. "A shame! Hopefully Salurean will be pleased with the acquisition of this robot. Take it to the brig and have him locked up."

The hulking machine slung Commander Candle over his shoulder and carried him down the corridor.

"When do I get to meet Salurean?" asked the Guardian.

"Once he is back from his mission to the Protector", answered the construct. Then it paused to become thoughtful.

"You are not deactivated!"

"No, but now you are!"

Commander Candle's fists hammered down on the goliath's head. The Death Droid dropped him. A thunderous punch sent the huge android through the bulkhead. A second sent it out into space. Commander Candle followed up his advantage by rocketing through the Death Droid's chest. The huge robot split into several pieces that simply began to drift in space.

Salurean's craft was left with a gaping hole in its side. It listed as oxygen fed flame burst from within. The smoke was sucked out into space.

"Thanks for the free ride to Salurean's ship!" exclaimed the commander. He streaked back to the pirate's craft and crashed through the bridge. Even as an energy shield sealed the further escape of interior pressure, Commander Candle easily overcame the bridge crew. He next turned his attention to the flight controls.

"We will see how far this craft can go once it dumps its reactor core!"

Content with his work, he flew out of the damaged craft and out into the interstellar region.

"The power surge was helpful, but the trip in outer space seem to get me fully charged," stated Daria to himself, "all I needed was a good dose of unfiltered sunshine and the absence of activity! A nap in the cosmos! And now for my meeting with Salurean on the Protector"

As he rocketed away from the enemy craft, it exploded.

* * *

The Admiral, Horatio, Gaius and the scientist entered the conference room.

"May I introduce Councilman Snillosh. You know Prince Gaius. This is Horatio Boaracious and Professor Jeremiah Hawks.

"How have you been, Ted?" asked his former teacher.

Snillosh looked at the professor as he strolled into the ready room. His pale green skin and flowing black hair concealed his identity as an earthman. However, his other features were unaltered except for his age.

"I have made a life for myself, just as you have, Professor Hawks."

He sat down. Gaius, the Admiral, Horatio, Camille. Elvis and Vermis were seated as well.

"You know envoy Snillosh?"

"Yes, I do Admiral. He was once my lab assistant on Earth. He was teleported here with me. His name is Ted Collins."

"Another Earthman!" exclaimed Gaius.

"I didn't think you just disappeared, Ted. Since the LaTruba alphabet has its 'C' pronounced like the 'sh' sound, it does not take a genius to realize that 'Snillosh' is simply your name spelled backwards."

"But why the deception?" asked Gaius. "You presented yourself as an Outerworld merchant to my brother."

"I did not want the attention Jeremiah Hawks has been receiving. After hooking up with that incompetent pirate, Jock LaFeet, I needed to become less recognizable or face prison for the few acts of piracy that actually went right! I saw an opportunity to provide leadership on LaTruba Two and benefited greatly from the trade alliance between Wakuhn and the Chitin Collective. I was doing quite well until they took over my adopted home. But, that is enough about me. It's time to tell you of my mission."

"Which is?" the admiral asked.

"I am to see that the fleet is deployed for the liberation of LaTruba Two. I am also to conduct Jeremiah Hawks to his meeting with the king."

"Hmm," groaned Destrada thoughtfully. "I think not; on both counts!"

"You would defy the king's written orders?"

"Sure. I've done it before. Sometimes he issues a command before he has all of the available intelligence. If I feel I do not have time to inform him, I act in the best interests of the Empire."

"That's preposterous!" protested Ted. "This is my home we are talking about!" Ted Collins rose defiantly.

"Not really. Our best intelligence tells us that the Chitins have pulled out of LaTruba Two! Now, envoy Snillosh, perhaps you can confirm the Chitin's current location?"

"Are you basing all of this speculation on pathetic mining droid's information? I heard about this so called informer from LaTruba Two."

"No," answered Prince Gaius. "An ODF officer is currently attacking the Chitin formation's rear flank with a retrofitted dreadnaught."

"And Ted," added Jeremiah Hawks, "the balance of the Wakuhnian fleet has cut off the advance upon Skyport. Once Salurean attacked my lab on the Terra-Quest we realized that there was a repeating pattern. After an attempt is made to neutralize me, then Skyport is assaulted."

An officer entered the briefing room and saluted the commanding officer.

"The Chitin fleet has been engaged, sir. We took them by surprise, and we are simply crushing them. Salurean's ship has been destroyed as reported by the dreadnaught commanded by Jock LaFeet."

"That's good news, eh Ted?"

"Yes, yes. I see that the king did not have all of the intelligence needed for an informed decision."

"A good thing too," stated the prince. "Because I happen to believe that someone has been giving Salurean military secrets, someone inside the inner counsel; someone like you!"

Ted Collins rose to his feet.

"You are speaking to a royal envoy! How dare you? Professor, are you going to stand for this?"

"Ted, it does seem to fit the facts. You are the one opposed to the movement to reform the treatment of the Zinj. Your first visit to the king happened right after the appearance of the mysterious pirate, Salurean. I find these facts particularly incriminating. My only question is this: are you Salurean or do you just work for him?"

Security personnel positioned themselves right behind Ted Collins.

"Arrest him!" commanded the admiral.

Ted struck the one guard and quickly relieved the other of his gun. Then he grabbed Jeremiah Hawks and held the pistol to his head.

"I demand safe conduct to my shuttle, or I'll kill the professor!"

"Ignore him Admiral. He intends to kill me anyway," stated Jeremiah Hawks.

"No. You're more valuable to Salurean alive!" countered Ted.

"I think not. I would never cooperate with him. Make your move Admiral."

Ted Collins backed up with the scientist toward the exit. As he did, the door opened. Commander Candle stood there and quickly grabbed and crushed the Mark IV in the Earthman's hand. He then grasped Ted Collins and held him in a headlock.

"The Guardian!" exclaimed Horatio.

"You're alive!" Jeremiah Hawks did not know whether to embrace him or not.

"Thanks to you, Professor, I am more alive than you know."

"That voice!" said Jeremiah Hawks softly.

"Everyone out!" shouted Daria. "Get out now!" Commander Candle dove forward and placed himself atop of Ted Collins.

The room cleared. Just as the admiral sealed the door, there was a massive explosion from within the room. The professor and the company he was with were flung backward by the concussion. Each fell to the floor in the fetal position, covering their eyes from flying debris.

Smoke swirled. Wires and ceiling tiles fell from above randomly. Amidst the fog a lone figure stepped out from what used to be the Protector of the Realm's ready room. Commander Candle was brushing the dust from himself.

"I felt his temperature spike. He was wired to blow."

"Did he do this or was it done by a signal?" asked the fleet's commander.

"Your sensors should be able to tell us that, Admiral", answered the Guardian. "Is everyone all-right?"

"I have a wicked headache, if anyone is interested", stated Horatio. He did not receive an answer from the others who were painfully rising.

"I didn't think anyone was" he laughed.

"What about Ted?" the professor queried.

"He was vaporized."

"But you are okay?" he asked Commander Candle.

"I am just fine! I have a track record for surviving fusion bomb blasts. But I do have a bit of a headache, too, Horatio Boaracious."

"Aren't you the being who saved Skyport Seven?" asked Gaius. "Who are you?"

"I am called Commander Candle. That is all you need to know right now. As a Guardian, my mission is to protect the Oracle and its keeper. Defending Skyport became an important part of my mission."

"And what is your mission now?' asked the prince.

"I am assigned to Jeremiah Hawks."

The academic glanced at his sentinel.

"That voice" he whispered. "I know you, don't I?"

"We will speak later, Professor! I will disclose everything privately, just between you and me."

A second officer entered the conference room.

"Sir, the fleet reports that the Chitin attack force has been neutralized. Over twenty ships have been destroyed and the rest have warped out of the sector. Our casualties have been very light and very little damage to any of the fleet."

"That is excellent news! Is there any word of Salurean?"

"A shuttle left the Protector moments before I came on board. I felt pressed to attend to Professor Hawks, so I made no effort to detain it" stated Commander Candle.

"Tell the bridge to track that shuttle, Ensign!"

"Yes sir!"

"Today has been a great victory for the Empire!" announced Destrada. "I thank each of you here for contributing to our safety and security. After we assess and mourn our losses, I would like us to convene for a victory celebration at Skyport Seven. I hear that Hume DeTosis can throw a good party, and I for one would like to experience his hospitality."

"I will see that he gets your request", volunteered Boaracious.

Technicians flooded the room to begin the repair of the damage. As Destrada led his officers to the bridge, the scientist stayed behind to talk with the Guardian.

"Commander Candle?"

"Yes, that is my new name, Professor."

"I recognize your voice. You are Espwin Daria! How did you survive the attack on my laboratory?"

"It was a sovereign act of God. I somehow merged with this robot before the explosion destroyed your complex."

"But you were critically wounded!"

"I feel fine, now," Daria spoke with a smile. The two men laughed. Then the professor began to cry.

"I guess I am too used to losing people close to me. I was thinking the worst!"

"It did look pretty bad, Professor. But don't blame yourself. Maybe, just maybe this is God's way of telling you that you have not lost the other people as well." The scientist looked up at his friend.

"Yes," he said softly by with conviction. "Yes! But how did you awaken?"

"At first I broke out of the Nultron housing and found a power coupling. Then, I feigned unconsciousness so the Death Droid would take me back to Salurean. Direct sunlight charges me up rather quickly, even in interstellar space. When I am active, I run an energy deficit. I need quiet time and un-refracted light to recharge to capacity."

"Not unlike a Christian, Daria."

"Amen to that, Professor. But I must be frank. I am troubled by my appearance. The Guardian's body seems to be similar to a description of the Lord in Revelations and other parts of Scripture. I am unsettled by this, and at the same time have a great sense of being unworthy."

"The Word of God says that we will be like Him when he appears, Daria. Also, though you have been blessed with a glorious body, it still does not compare with His, nor will it compare with any of ours at the resurrection. Besides, it is clear that you are quite limited in power. The power of God is limitless. Several times we were forced to minister to you in an inactive state."

"Thank you, Professor! The Lord is not weary nor does He faint! I guess I have the privilege of reflecting just a small amount of His glory."

"All believers should, Espwin Daria! In your instance you have a warrior's calling."

"So, where do we go to now?" asked the commander.

"I think Horatio wants to see Hume DeTosis about arranging a victory celebration for the admiral. By the way, can you still eat? The mayor throws a good party!"

"I don't know! I don't need to. As far as a party is concerned, my concept of a good time has changed significantly these past few weeks!"

Chapter Ten: Tomorrow is a Star Lit Sky

"Something bad happened here!" stated Elvis. Camille stood somberly at his side atop the wreckage that was once the parliamentary building of LaTruba Two. Dust swirled. The hot red sun broiled down upon the ruins and scorched soil of what was once a prosperous city.

"Is there anything or anyone left?"

"Only inhabitants of the remotely populated areas," answered Camille. "Other than that, we cannot account for the two billion people who once lived on this planet."

A communicator squelched.

"Commander Elvis! I have a survivor! A small child! He was hiding in the sewers, and claims that there may be more down there!"

"Bring the child to the mobile HQ. After I interview him we will assign four squads to conduct a search."

"There's hope!" said Camille as she sighed.

"Indeed. Let's hope that our forward scouts find out something when they scan the terra-formed planet we graciously gave to the Chitins when they first appeared."

"I agree. I want us to bring back all of the information we can to the professor. He told us that there will be a special meeting."

*   *   *

"Captain," reported a Striker pilot. He entered the bridge area and saluted. The senior officer stood gazing into the forward monitor with his hands clasped behind his back as he stood. He turned. It was Prince Gaius. He was the new captain of the Royal Crest.

"Yes Lieutenant Quint. Did your group discover anything?"

"Sir, the planet has been abandoned. It has been stripped clean! There was no vegetation, and no dwellings. A landing party found underground catacombs. They were crude, sir. There was no technology to speak of. Our examination of the site is over. For the rest, I think we need a team of biologists."

"No civilization? Are you suggesting that the Chitins lived in these primitive dwellings? Then how did they get use of their space craft? Who made these for them?"

"Sir, I am just telling you what we found. The area is secure enough to have the Royal Crest use planetary scanners. Sir, we found what we found!"

"Please carry on Lieutenant Quint.. Please keep a couple of scouts active. That should serve our security purposes."

"Yes sir!"

The junior officer saluted and left. Concern and perplexity furrowed deep into the heart of the prince. If they are not here or on LaTruba Two, where have they gone? Did we get them all?" he asked himself.

One of the many bridge officers called out.

"Captain, I have a call on the com for you, sir."

"Gaius here," he answered after he pressed a communication console.

"Professor Hawks, my prince. I believe that you have heard the news about LaTruba Two?

"Yes, Jeremiah. I am afraid we are coming up with more of the same. Can this be?"

"I will not speculate, particularly if we cannot guarantee a secure com-link. I am preparing for a meeting at an undisclosed location. Admiral Destrada has granted me permission to have you there. It did not take very much convincing, I might add."

"When will we meet?"

"In two weeks. I will be counting on you to do the speaking."

"I'll be there. Hopefully we will have more information by then."

"The Chitin's activities have been mysterious, Prince Gaius. I do hope we can gain enough intelligence to avoid another attack!"

* * *

"You are stable" announced the professor. He stood amidst a massive new laboratory. The patient chair rotated revealing a more handsomely structured Alexander Tweed. Several months had passed since the second successful defense of Skyport.

"You never cease to amaze me, Professor. Not only have you rescued me from the brink of death, I am now a more efficiently engineered machine! I only wish," he paused as he became teary eyed, "that we partnered as we should have on Earth. My wealth and your resourcefulness could have done much good!"

"Alexander, we were both too unfocused to grasp the opportunity. Besides, we're here now. It seems like God is getting His way with us. I can't take any of the credit for that!"

"That's right you old bag of bolts!" commented an elderly gentleman.

"Pappy Ernest, how are you? Thank you for allowing the Professor use of your secret base. The laboratory facilities have been exceptional!" stated Alexander.

"Yessiree! When I was alone here for twenty years, I just couldn't stop building things! I'm happy to see my base go to such a good use!"

"How do you feel Alexander?" interrupted Jeremiah Hawks.

"I desperately need to dig something! I'm still a mining drone. Do you need a shaft somewhere?"

"Follow me, sonny! You're speaking my language now. I want to rework some of our hangar access, and can use some work on the far quarter."

Pappy and Alexander moved to their new task. Elvis and Camille entered the lab area.

"Professor Hawks! You've got to see this!" raved Camille.

"Yeah," Elvis supported her enthusiasm. "Jock's father has designed a bunch of ships! He has plans drawn to further incorporate Nultron technology to the various classes of the Wakuhnian fleet."

"Improving the Strikers even more!" continued Camille. "He has even designed new Striker armor! You just have to review these plans!"

"I will. Remember the staff meeting in half an hour. Prince Gaius will be there to update us on some recent developments."

"We'll be there," they answered. Then they both ran off like children who had a pocket full of candy.

Commander Candle was flying about the cavernous ceiling. He spotted the scientist and his mentor in the Bible and landed in front of him.

"I'm done."

"Done?"

"Yes, I realized how I can protect the Oracle and you even if they are in two different locations," claimed Daria.

"How is that?" asked Jeremiah Hawks.

"I have committed the Oracle and the Bible to memory! Now I won't have to choose between protecting you and the Oracle! It's in my mind!

"That's ingenious! Now let me ask you something. Doesn't this bring up a new conflict? What if you have to choose between protecting me and saving yourself?"

"Yikes, I didn't think of that!"

"Please resolve that philosophical question, and let me know. But I think you are on the, right track. Still I would focus on the Bible studies I have been supplying you as well as your own prayer and study."

"I intend to do that Professor. I am concerned that I may have programming that I cannot override with my own thinking. There is no paradox with me! Now that I know that the Oracle can be reproduced, I am not overly apprehensive about the book itself as I am about my mission to protect you."

"With all of the copies of the Bible and the Oracle in publication, prayerfully, the least of your worries will be protecting our originals," added the former academic.

"That is fortunate, that the Word of God is available and not locked up in a cave somewhere!. When is the meeting?"

"In about twenty minutes. I'm heading for the auditorium now."

A head suddenly appeared through the floor below.

"Yeeow!" exclaimed the scientist. "Vermis, you have to stop doing that!" The worm-like friend of the professor wiggled out of the hole and stood.

"I am sorry, Professor Hawks. Horatio wants me to chart where the sub floor is supported by loose dust instead of rock. This is the best way of doing that. He plans to reinforce wherever the foundation seems weak."

"You may want to take a break. We have a staff meeting soon!"

"I know! Prince Gaius will be there. I wouldn't want to miss it!" Vermis dove back into the hole and within seconds disappeared. Horatio waved to the scientist from another station.

"Let's see what Horatio wants," said Jeremiah to Commander Candle.

"I will follow you, Professor."

It was a short walk. Soon they were at the porker's side.

"Take a look at this, Professor. If we can engineer some deep space freight transfers, I believe that we can keep this base's location somewhat secret. Our main manufacturing facility will remain on Skyport. I will have a direct and secure line established so we can be assured of private communication."

"That should be satisfactory. Do you think Hume DeTosis will cooperate with the deep space transfers?"

"I have already talked with him. He's happy to have the plant and jobs located on Skyport. The idea that your design laboratory is elsewhere will minimize any future attacks on his home. He is happy about that too. He did make it a point to say that he wants you to visit regularly, though. I am working with General Kur-Dan an emergency response protocol in case we need the ODF to assist us."

"Good work Horatio. I am hoping that we can benefit from this marvelous base for many years and not be worried about any attacks on it."

"The real issue is to have people here we can trust, boss. We need people who won't sell us out."

"Manta will bring people," spoke a voice from behind. The three turned to see the aged Zinj. Jeremiah Hawks ran up to embrace him.

"You gained leave to come! I am so glad to see you!"

"I came with Prince Gaius. Master Tolem insisted. He sends his greetings."

"What did you mean when you said that you would send people?" asked Horatio.

"Twenty Zinj have volunteered to come. They have their master's blessing."

"That's wonderful!" exclaimed Jeremiah Hawks. "More and more Wakuhnians are working within the law to make the Zinj as free as possible!"

Manta drew close to Commander Candle.

"The Guardian!" he exclaimed. Then he knelt and bowed.

"There is no need to show reverence," stated Commander Candle. "I am not a celestial being. I am a just a servant like you, assigned to protect the Oracle and its keeper Jeremiah Hawks." The commander grasped the Zinj's hands and guided him to his feet.

Suddenly a holographic image appeared in front of the professor. It was Ian, Daria's computerized assistant.

"Staff meeting in ten minutes" he announced.

"This is Ian. He was sent to me because he needed severe repair. He had four books of the Bible in his memory. Someone made the mistake of asking him to analyze it. He's been caught in an infinite analytical loop ever since!"

"Professor" whispered Daria, "I did that! He used to be my navigator!"

Jeremiah Hawks turned to the holograph. "Go ahead of us. We'll be right there!"

"He has been having problems for years. I may have to wipe out his memory just to get him to cancel the analysis command and function normally. After all, the Bible was never meant for computer analysis. The natural mind cannot comprehend it. Anyway, let's go. I don't want to be late," said the professor.

"I'll give you a lift!" offered Commander Candle. Seconds later, he held the scientist as he flew across the cavernous room. Horatio and Manta waved below.

The resident staff scurried into the makeshift auditorium. Prince Gaius stood at the podium. The meeting began.

"I thank you fellow believers for allowing me this special time. I am very happy to inform you that the Zinj Captivity and Repression Reform Act has been passed by the Imperial Senate and signed into law by my brother. It is a great step forward in the fight to liberate the Zinj and restore them to equality in our culture."

There was a contagious applause. The prince motioned this to silence with his hands.

"I do have disturbing news, however. The evidence gathered from LaTruba Two and the Chitin's original colony did not grant us much information. We know that a sizeable portion of their fleet did retreat and escape our last confrontation.

"While there are many unanswered questions, even about the Chitin's use of the technology necessary for space travel. One certain thing remains. We have an adversary with a sizeable fleet that is at large and to this point undetected. We can only assume that our enemy is preparing to strike.

"Likewise, we have not been able to track the shuttle used by Salurean to escape during the second battle for Skyport. He likewise, has vanished and we have not had any pirate activity attributed to him or any of his former associates.

"We also have done extensive analysis of the explosion caused by envoy Snillosh when he failed to escape our custody. This is rather disturbing news. While we presumed that the envoy was vaporized, enough genetic samples were available to run tests. The envoy that was with us that day was not an earthman, but a clone. His DNA was only a 95% match."

The professor scratched his head. "He had me fooled!"

"While the Wakuhnian armada and the ODF maintain vigilance," continued Gaius, "we need to be prepared to support their activity to the best of our ability. In addition, I am here today to propose a new project. We want to restore communications with the now indigenous Zinj of Earth. Using that technology that sent Professor Hawks to our sector, we will attempt to contact the Zinj on Earth and seek to restore our fellowship with them. This has great spiritual significance, since there will be events on Earth that will mark the return of Jesus Christ. We also will require their assistance in monitoring the threat posed by the Chitins. Our next goal, then, is to establish contact with Earth!"

The assembly cheered. Jeremiah Hawks cried and hoped. "Perhaps, just perhaps," thought the professor, "Daria was right. Perhaps he could hear some news about his family!

* * *

The detective leaned back on his chair as the video narrative came to its conclusion.

"This is a fantastic story! If I was desperately searching for my heritage I may want to believe it and pay handsomely for more information," he stated.

"Who said I was selling it? I have something else in mind."

"Which is?"

"The opportunity to see Jeremiah Hawks in person, the chance to know your father."

"I know my Father. I gave my heart to Jesus Christ many years ago. I have accepted the tragedy to my family's break-up and subsequent foster care as God's provision for my life. It has helped me come to Him and has been integral in making me the person I am today."

"I believe that as well. I also believe that He made you into the world's greatest investigator for the very task I am suggesting. The contingent I represent is preparing to contact Wakuhn. We need to send someone who will be able to negotiate Wakuhnian society, and arrange a meeting with Jeremiah Hawks. You will be the most acceptable candidate. Your father will meet with you because of who you are. Your appearance will substantiate the contact from Earth. It's not just about contacting your father. Several planetary systems and maybe Earth itself hang in the balance."

Jeremy Hawks pondered this pronouncement. Having benefited from a couple of space shuttle flights, he had become familiar with the possibilities held secret in the cosmos.

"Why do you want me to do this? What is in it for you?"

"What is in it for me? Nothing but more anxious moments and more sleepless nights," the woman lamented. Her companion suddenly turned on the light. She removed the large hat that helped conceal her features. Her escort removed his coat to reveal the frame of a mature male Zinj.

Jeremy Hawks looked into the eyes of a woman he had not seen since he was a very young child.

"It can't be! I was told that you were dead!"

"I'm not. Now that I have found you, my son, I do not want to risk losing you, too. But the man I love, your father, needs your help. He has been under constant attack since his arrival on Luna One. I know that you will be able to do what your father has been unable to, that is, find Salurean. I believe that God has prepared you for this very moment."

"Why did you wait until now, to make contact?"

"I was severely injured the night of the fire, son. I was rescued by a Zinj as I was being strangled in our basement. In the scuffle to save my life, the fire started, and I was taken, unconscious, into the custody and company of the Zinj. For five years I was in a coma. By then you were all placed, and I could only get my children back at the expense of exposing the Zinj's secret operations here on Earth."

Jeremy Hawks stood and walked over to his mother. He embraced her.

"I am so sorry, mom. It must have been hard for you."

"That is not important, now, son. Will you go?" she asked.

"I want to pray. I want to get some opinions of people I truly respect. I may also have to ask a girl to put off a wedding."

"I understand. We have some time. The teleportation device is still under construction."

"I will get what I need done quickly. How will I contact you?"

"Use this," Jeremy's mother handed him a small golden coin. "Press here. You will receive a location where we will meet with you."

Jeremy nodded his assent.

"Remember this saying, 'Tomorrow is a star lit sky'. It will be our confirmation."

"Are there other players?" asked the detective.

"I hope not. If so it is later than we think."

His mother and Zinj escort bundled back up and left the office. Jeremy watched from his window as they left his building and made their way on the street below.

"Tomorrow is a star lit sky!" he repeated. He shook his head in disbelief, worry and some old fashioned investigative intuition. "There are other players, Mom. Thank God He's always on time!"

The sleuth retrieved his hat and coat and prepared himself to brave the cold. He grinned slightly. As a seasoned investigator he always knew what cases he would take. It never had anything to do with money or prestige or even the person who sought him out; he just knew.

Jeremy Hawks was already on this case!

www.ingramcontent.com/pod-product-compliance
Ingram Content Group UK Ltd.
Pitfield, Milton Keynes, MK11 3LW, UK
UKHW020128250726
13967UKWH00002B/536